PLANTS AND FLOWERS IN THE HOME

A Golden Hands book

Marshall Cavendish, London

Authors: Elizabeth Gundry, Cynthia Wickham

Illustrator: Sue Richards

Photographers
A-Z collection, Barnaby's Picture Library, Steve Bicknell, Michael Boys, Heididi Carstenson, Alan Duns, David Hicks, R. Kalvar/Camera Press, Chris Lewis, Bill McLaughlin, Brian Morris, M. Newton, Popperphoto, Ursula Rellstab Haller, Sale/Stone/Senior, Scoop, Miki Slingsby, Harry Smith, Colin Watmough, Elizabeth Whiting, Michael Wickham, ZEFA

Arrangements and Designs
Stella Coe, Flower House, Elizabeth Gundry, Dawn Marsden, Pullbrooke and Gould, John Stefanidis

Published by Marshall Cavendish Publications Limited
58 Old Compton Street
London W1V 5PA

© Marshall Cavendish Limited 1973/1974
58 Old Compton Street
London W1V 5PA

Part of this material was first published
by Marshall Cavendish Limited in the Specials:
Flowers and Plants in the Home
Arranging Flowers and growing House Plants

This volume first printed 1974

ISBN 0 85685 062 4

About this book . . .

You don't need a large garden to enjoy the pleasure which plants and flowers give. The hundreds of ideas in this book guarantee success for the most amateur indoor gardener and ensure that those big-city blues are banished the year round.

The first section of this colour-packed book is devoted to flowers—how to grow, pick, prepare and arrange them. There are detailed guides to the various styles used by professional flower-arrangers—from simple cottage styles to really sophisticated arrangements for those special occasions.

And for the more ambitious there are pages devoted to new and exciting ways to decorate with flowers and other material. Try your hand at Ikebana—the delicate Oriental art of flower arranging—or learn how to dry and display those short-lived summer blooms.

The final half of the book is devoted to plants in the home—from colourful bulbs to giant tropical plants. The best methods of displaying them are fully explained and illustrated and special attention is given to planning a total look with plants—one that will enhance every room in your home.

But that isn't all. There are plants to use in hanging baskets; miniature gardens; cacti; and fruits to grow from pips and stones. You can learn how to grow Bonsai and how to plan a bottle garden or Wardian case. And to make sure your plants stay healthy we've included pages on care and how to propagate your plants successfully.

The great thing about Plants and Flowers in the Home is that all the ideas and skills it so colourfully describes are both easy to learn and inexpensive. For the armchair-gardener it's a must.

Contents

bringing flowers and plants into the home

Flowers and plants make any home come to life—they bring sunshine and freshness to a city room, a promise of spring to dark winter nights, and summer sweetness to a country window-sill. Part of the poignant charm of cut flowers lies in the fact that they will only be with you for a week or two—but if the expense or the heartbreak is too much, then a sturdy pot plant or a jar of dried grasses will keep you company for months.

Flowers in the home should look relaxed and natural, not stiffly formal like hotel foyer arrangements. Sometimes it pays to pick a colour that works well with other colours in the room—pink Lilies against a soft, sherry-coloured wall; a mass of multi-coloured Polyanthus on a mahogany table; a group of lush green plants against white, white walls or a mirror.

In halls and on landings

Passage ways are often sadly neglected, which makes it all the more pleasant to be greeted by a handsome jardinière or a bucket of country flowers.

If your hall is draughty and pot plants blench every time the front door is opened, dried flowers make a beautiful alternative. Just remember to re-arrange them occasionally so they don't become static, dull and dusty.

On a landing, a window with a dreary outlook can be turned into a miniature greenhouse with glass shelves, trailing plants and any pretty pieces of translucent, coloured glass you can find.

In the living room

Many modern homes have no fireplace. Instead, you could re-arrange your sofas and chairs and make your focal point a low table with a tray of flowers and plants. As you change the cut flowers, or as a pot plant comes into bloom or unfurls a new leaf, so you have a constantly changing, living focal point.

Otherwise, a group of pot plants in the fireplace looks effective—but choose plants that don't need a lot of light.

In the dining room

Even if you have dried flowers elsewhere, try to have fresh flowers on the dining table, kept low so everyone can talk without having to peer round the vase. Or, for special parties, put an individual nosegay by every place setting—perhaps Snowdrops, Gentians, or Forget-me-nots. If flower heads like Roses have broken off short, float them in a shallow bowl and stand slender, creamy candles among them.

In bedrooms

There's an alarmist theory that dozens of flowers and plants busily breathing oxygen during the night can make a room airless. But a single Rose on a dressing table, or a little posy of Violets beside a bed makes a thoughtful touch.

In the bathroom

Many plants love the steamy atmosphere of bathrooms (it reminds them of their jungly origins).

The main thing about flowers and plants is to love them and care for them properly—if you do, they will repay you by making your home friendly, alive and welcoming.

a flower garden for picking

Any garden or flower bed which is planted primarily for picking should, obviously, produce as many flowers in variety for as long as possible and also be attractive in its own right.

Flowers for picking must, of course, actually like being picked, and enjoy a week or so in water in the house. And Nature is so generous that most of them do, particularly if you pick them carefully and at the right time. Blooms which have died should be removed to encourage the plant to flower again, otherwise it will expend its energy making seed.

Colour

The ideal bed for picking contains annuals and perennials, together with plants and shrubs for cutting for their foliage colours. But there is also the question of what colour flowers to grow. Naturally this is more a matter of personal taste than anything else, and depends upon which colours you feel you want to see in your living-room.

A bed for cutting is, however, incomplete without some of the silver-grey foliage plants which complement all colours, both vivid and subtle. (They also do a lot to tone down red brick in a garden.)

Do not forget that any colour is intensified by a touch of white, or a tiny accent of its opposite colour. (This is as true in the growing border as in the container.) So do not limit yourself to growing flowers in shades of one colour.

Which flowers to grow?

When choosing what to plant for picking you should, therefore, first decide which colours you want to include. But you must also, of course, think about the heights and flowering seasons of the plants. If you suddenly find that the only two flowers available for cutting are, say, a midget and a giant you will have great problems filling your containers.

The flower arranger who has a garden as brimming with colour as this one has no problem in finding suitable blooms for cutting. However, with a little careful planning, even the smallest garden will produce a wealth of blooms to give you cut flowers the whole year round.

The chart on pages 14–17 lists, according to their colour, suitable flowers for picking and gives their approximate heights and flowering seasons. But consult your seedsman or nursery, too, for more accurate details on the varieties of plants which are available in your area. Some of the flowers listed on the chart may be ones which you have not previously considered picking—try them, they are all lovely in vases.

Growing from seed

Growing flowers from seed is not always a trouble-free occupation. Hardy and half-hardy annuals in particular are not the easiest things to grow—they need care, good soil, plenty of light and water. There is nothing to be gained by buying a packet of seeds and scattering it about on a piece of dry, weedy soil—you might just as well give up, or wait to buy bedding plants at a shop. Gardening is not entirely easy and care-free, and you must care for and love the plants and treat them well.

Growing perennials

Perennials are bought as plants from nurseries or garden centres and can also be grown from seed. They live for years, dying down in winter and coming up again in the spring. In late autumn mark their place with a label or stick, it is amazing how easy it is to have forgotten where they are by spring.

They are generally sown during the summer in a well-dug and prepared seed bed. If the weather is dry they must be well-watered. In temperate climates the smaller seeds should be sown in a greenhouse or propagator at 13°-18°C (55°-65°F) in seed compost in spring. Many perennials sown this early will flower and can be picked the same summer—Hollyhocks, Asters and *Aquilegia* (Columbine) for example. The seedlings should be carefully pricked out into a frame or protected bed and after three to five months they can go into their permanent positions. Many, naturally, can be bought as plants, but the best way of all to acquire plants is from friends' gardens.

When your perennials are firmly established remember that large clumps need lifting and dividing every two to three years.

Growing hardy biennials

These can be sown in a greenhouse in a temperature of 13°C (55°F), or in a prepared seed bed in the garden in early summer. Keep the seedlings well-watered and in early autumn, when they have grown into bushy, plump little plants, plant them out into their places for spring. Some, such as Wallflowers, Brompton Stock and Iceland Poppies will flower in their first year if sown early. (Poppies should go on seeding themselves.)

Growing hardy annuals

These can be sown into seed boxes in seed compost but are more usually sown into their flowering positions in a well-prepared bed. The ground should have been dug over in the winter and forked and raked to a fine tilth (that is, with no lumps). Seeds are sown evenly in fairly dry soil in late spring, raked lightly over and watered with a fine rose on the watering can (too rough a spurt of water might knock them right out of the ground). Water them every day if the weather is dry and hot. When the seedlings come up close together thin them out when they are two or three inches high, to about three-quarters of their ultimate height apart. (If for example they will grow to a height of two feet, then plant them 18 inches away from each other.)

Growing half-hardy annuals

These are, of course, not as easy to grow as the hardy varieties, and could be bought from a nursery early in the summer as plants.

Sow the seeds in pots or seed boxes in spring, in a heated greenhouse, frame or propagator, and keep the soil moist at all times. Prick the seedlings out into a box of potting compost (about 30-35 to a box) holding them by their leaves and never touching or disturbing the roots. Then keep them somewhere warm and protected.

When all danger of frost is past gradually harden off the seedlings. Put them outside in the open in a sheltered spot in their boxes during the day, and return them to their warm protected quarters at night. In early summer plant them out in the bed.

flowering shrubs and trees

One of the best times of the year to think about using sprays of flowering trees and shrubs to enliven your home is when the bare brown twigs of winter start to bud into the flowers and leaves of spring. At this season they are doubly valuable—there is not much else available for room decoration, and there are few things nicer than watching their leaves and buds open out.

Because of their strong, sculptural forms many flowering shrubs lend themselves particularly well to a simple and effective flower arrangement where curves, angles, and natural growing shapes are vitally important. To make a long-lasting display, remember that all shrub and tree stems need to be crushed, split, peeled and given a good drink before arranging. And strip off about half the leaves, particularly the largest ones, as they crowd the container and detract from the beauty of the blossoms or flowers.

Blossom

Fruit blossom, like any woody-stemmed plant, needs a little extra care to ensure a reasonably long-lived arrangement. Blossom should always be cut when the buds are tight, and either early in the morning or in the evening. If it is cut early in the spring before there is much sign of life at all the buds will open in the warmth of the house. It is particularly important to keep flowering blossoms out of a draught. And remember that all woody-stemmed flowers need crushing or smashing at the base, or slitting up an inch or so, so that they can absorb enough water. Then give

Cherry blossom—sweet-scented but fragile

them a long drink in a cool, dark place before you arrange them. Use only three or four stems in an arrangement so that their shape can be appreciated.

Plum blossom is usually the earliest fruit tree to appear, and after it come Cherry, Apple, Quince, and Pear blossom. Even with the greatest care these blossoms will not last as long in water as Roses or Daisies, but their beauty more than compensates for their short life.

Evergreens

Many of the evergreens like Bay, Laurel, Holly, and Privet are good for spring and winter decoration.

Shrubs

Most types of *Clematis* (Virgin's Bower) are superb, and very graceful with their trailing stars of pink, white, and purple.

Forsythia (Golden Bells) with its yellow starry flowers, closely followed by brilliant green leaves, is one of the shrubs whose branches can be cut when the buds are only just showing. It will come into flower in the house.

Jasmin Nudiflorum (Winter Jasmine) is very useful indoors because, as its name suggests, it flowers continuously throughout the dreary winter months. In England it is well worth considering at Christmas time as its fresh yellow flowers contrast well with the Holly and the Ivy and their dark green leaves.

Perhaps the most wonderful of all flowering shrubs are the various varieties of *Lonicera* (Honeysuckle) which fall into graceful shapes and fill the entire house with scent.

Philadelphus (or 'Mock Orange') with its heady, sweet scent is also rewarding to cut and bring indoors. Strip most of the leaves off so that the water can reach the flowers and is not all taken up by the leaves. (This, incidentally, is a shrub which should be pruned after flowering.)

Ribes Sanguinium (Flowering Currant) is another good spring subject. The twigs, like those of *Forsythia*, can be cut and brought into the house at the end of winter. Their leaves and flowers will open in the room and fill it with scent.

Philadelphus is ideal for cutting

Sambucus (Elder) when picked in bud will fill the room with a sweet honey fragrance and the delicate lacy flowers are most decorative when they open.

Both because of its colour and scent *Syringa* (this is Lilac—not 'Mock Orange' as is sometimes thought) is worth cutting for the house. Most of the foliage must be stripped off the stems and the ends crushed.

Three more fragrant shrubs which are ideal for cutting while the buds are small are *Chimonanthus Fragrans* (Winter Sweet), *Hammemelis Mollis* (Witch Hazel), and *Mahonia Beali syn Mahonia Japonica* with its yellow flowers smelling of Lily-of-the-Valley.

Trees

Alder and Hazel are good cut to open in water as are all the Willows. The earlier you cut these the less dusting up of yellow pollen you will have to do, although this seems a small price to pay for the pleasure catkins give.

A great favourite to be cut on a country walk (but do not be too greedy, and be careful not to damage the tree) is *Aesculus Hippocastanum* (the Horse Chestnut) whose 'sticky buds' dramatically develop into marvellous pleated, brilliant green stars and flower buds.

Escallonia, a gum tree from the Chilian mountains, does well in sheltered gardens and is good for arrangements. It has dark, glossy leaves and rosy pink flowers.

Tall sprays of Forsythia stripped of its leaves make an arresting arrangement.

pick your own flowers

Latin name	Common name	Type	Height	Flowering season
White:				
Anaphalis	★ Pearl Everlasting	P	1-2ft	Summer
Convallaria Majalis	Lily-of-the-Valley, May Lily	P	6-12″	Early Summer
Yellow, orange, white:				
Achillea	★ Yarrow	P	2-5ft	Summer
Anthemis	Camomile	P	6″-2ft	Summer
Arctotis Decurrens	African Daisy	HHA	2ft	Summer
Calendula	★★Pot Marigold	HA	1½ft	Mid-Late Summer
Chrysanthemum Maximum	★★Shasta Daisy	P	1½ft	Summer
Dimorphotheca	Cape Daisy	HHA	1-3ft	Summer
Doronicum	★ Leopard's Bane	P	9″-3ft	Spring-Early Summer
Eschscholzia Californica	California Poppy	HA	1-2ft	Summer
Euphorbia	★★Spurge	P	1-2ft	Early Summer
Gazania	Treasure Flower	P	6-12″	Summer
Helenium	Sneezeweed	P	1½-5ft	Summer
Helianthus	★★Sunflower	P	3-5ft/12ft	Mid-Late Summer
Hesperis	Sweet Rocket	B/P	1-3ft	Summer
Mentzelia	Blazing Star	HA	1-2ft	Summer
*Narcissus	Daffodil or Narcissus	Bb	4″-2ft	Mid-Winter—Spring
Oenothera	Evening Primrose	B/P	6″-4ft	Summer
Papaver Nudicaule	Iceland Poppy	B	1½ft	Summer
Primula Vulgaris	★ Primrose	P	4″	Spring
Rudbeckia	★★Cone Flower	HA	2-3ft	Late Summer
Tagetes	★ Marigold	HHA	1-2ft	Summer
Tropaeolum Majus	★ Nasturtium	HA	6-9″	Late Summer

The Latin name Narcissus refers not only to the white flower commonly called Narcissus but also to the Daffodil which is a member of the same family.

Key to symbols used in the chart
Lasting time in water:
★ a week or more; ★★ longer
B – Biennial
Bb – Bulb
C – Corm

HA – Hardy Annual
HHA – Half-Hardy Annual
P – Perennial
S – Shrub

Perennials—plants which come up every year.

Latin name	Common name	Type	Height	Flowering season
Verbascum	Mullein	B/P	3-6ft	Summer
Pink, red, white:				
Acanthus Mollis	Bear's Breeches	P	3-4ft	Summer
Armeria	Thrift, Sea-pink	P	1½ft	Early Summer
Astrantia	★ Masterwort	P	1-3ft	Summer
Centranthus		HA/P	2-3ft	Mid-Summer
Cleome	Spider Flower	HHA/B	3-3½ft	Summer
Dainthus barbatus	★★Sweet William	B	8-18″	Late Spring—Early Summer
Godetia	★	HA	6″-2ft	Summer
Incarvillea	Chinese Trumpet Flower	P	1-1½ft	Early Summer
Lavatera	Tree Mallow	HA/B	2-2½ft	Summer
Lychnis	Campion	P	1½-3ft	Late Summer
Monarda Didyma	Sweet Bergamot, Bee Balm or Oswego Tea	P	1-2ft	Summer
Paeonia	★ Peony	P	2-3ft	Early Summer
Papaver Orientale	Oriental Poppy	P	2-4ft	Late Spring—Early Summer
Pyrethrum Roseum	★ Feverfew	P	2-3ft	Early Summer
Blue and white:				
Ageratum	★ Floss-flower	HHA	4-18″	Summer
Anchusa	★ Alkenet, Bugloss	P	15″-3ft	Spring—Early Summer
Aquiliega	★ Columbine	P	1-3ft	Early Summer
Campanula	★ Bellflower	B/P	4″-2½ft/3-6ft	Summer
Catananche	Cupid's Dart, Blue Cupidone	P	2ft	Summer
Delphinium	★	HA/P	3-5ft	Early Summer
Echinops	★★Globe Thistle	P	3½ft	Late Summer
Eryngium	★ Sea Holly	P	2ft	Late Summer
Linum	★ Flax	P	1-2ft	Late Spring

Biennials—plants sown in the summer to flower the following spring and available from nurseries and plant shops as well as growable from seed

Annuals—plants which grow, flower and die in one season and which are grown from seed or brought as plantlets.

N.B.—All plants are listed by type—hardy annual, half-hardy annual etc.— according to how they are grown in the temperate zones.

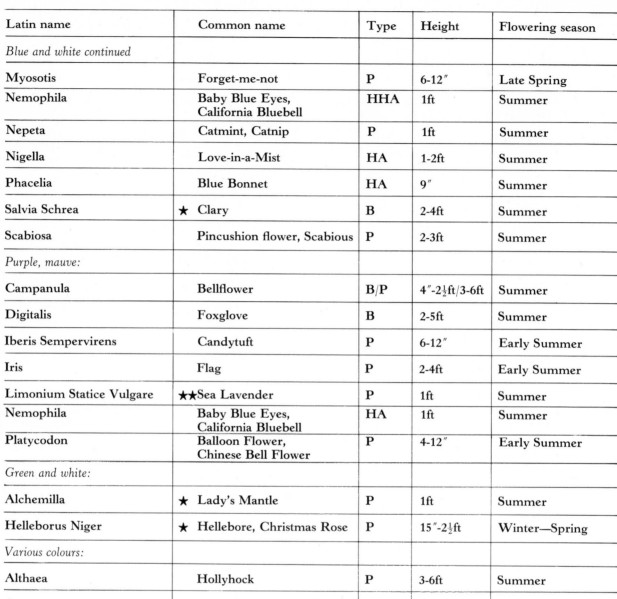

Latin name	Common name	Type	Height	Flowering season
Blue and white continued				
Myosotis	Forget-me-not	P	6-12″	Late Spring
Nemophila	Baby Blue Eyes, California Bluebell	HHA	1ft	Summer
Nepeta	Catmint, Catnip	P	1ft	Summer
Nigella	Love-in-a-Mist	HA	1-2ft	Summer
Phacelia	Blue Bonnet	HA	9″	Summer
Salvia Schrea	★ Clary	B	2-4ft	Summer
Scabiosa	Pincushion flower, Scabious	P	2-3ft	Summer
Purple, mauve:				
Campanula	Bellflower	B/P	4″-2½ft/3-6ft	Summer
Digitalis	Foxglove	B	2-5ft	Summer
Iberis Sempervirens	Candytuft	P	6-12″	Early Summer
Iris	Flag	P	2-4ft	Early Summer
Limonium Statice Vulgare	★★Sea Lavender	P	1ft	Summer
Nemophila	Baby Blue Eyes, California Bluebell	HA	1ft	Summer
Platycodon	Balloon Flower, Chinese Bell Flower	P	4-12″	Early Summer
Green and white:				
Alchemilla	★ Lady's Mantle	P	1ft	Summer
Helleborus Niger	★ Hellebore, Christmas Rose	P	15″-2½ft	Winter—Spring
Various colours:				
Althaea	Hollyhock	P	3-6ft	Summer
Anemone	★ Windflower	P	6-18″	Spring—Autumn
Antirrhinum	★ Snapdragon	HHA	6″-3ft	Summer—Autumn
Aster		P	1-3ft	Early-Late Summer
Aster Novae-belgii	Michaelmas Daisy, New York Aster	P	Up to 4ft	Autumn
Callisterphus	China Aster	HHA	9″-2ft	Summer
Centaurea Cyanus	★ Cornflower	HA	1-2½ft	Summer
Cheiranthus	Wallflower	B/P	6″-2ft	Mid-Spring—Summer
Clarkia		HA	1-4ft	Summer
Cosmos	★ Mexican Aster	HHA	2-3ft	Mid-Late Summer

Latin name	Common name	Type	Height	Flowering season
Chrysanthemum	★ Mums	HA	1-3ft	Summer
Dahlia	★	P	1-4ft/20ft	Summer—Autumn
Dianthus	★ Pinks	P	1ft	Early-Mid Summer
Dianthus Caryophyllus	Carnation	B	1-2ft	Late Summer
Gladiolus	Glads	C	1½ft-4ft	Mid-Spring—Summer
Helichrysum Bracteatum	★ Strawflower, Everlasting	HHA	2-3ft	Summer
Heuchera	Alum Root, Coral Bells	P	1-3ft	Summer
Lathyrus	Sweet Pea	HA	Up to 5ft	Summer
Lobelia		HHA	6"-3ft	Early-Late Summer
Matthiola	Stock, Gilliflower	B	1-2ft	Summer
Nemesia		HHA	4-12"	Summer
Nicotiana	Tobacco	HHA	1½-3ft	Summer
Pelargonium Zonale	Geranium	P	6"-3ft	Summer
Petunia		HHA	9-18"	Summer
Phlox	★ Flame Flower	P	6"-3ft	Mid-Late Summer
Ranunculus		P	4"-3ft	Late Winter—Summer
Salpiglossis	Painted Tongue	HHA	1½-2ft	Summer
Salvia	★ Sage	HA/P	1½-5ft.	Summer
Tulipa	Tulip	Bb	4"-2½ft	Spring
Verbena	Vervain	HHA	1-4ft	Summer
Viola		P	6"	Spring—Summer
Viola Tricolor	Pansy	B/P	6"	Spring—Summer
Zinnia	★★Youth and Old Age	HHA	1-3ft	Summer—Autumn
Grey, silver:				
Artemisia arborescens	Wormwood	P	3-5ft	Grown for foliage
Lavandula	Lavender	S	Up to 4ft	Grown for foliage
Ruta Graveolens	Rue, Herb of Grace	S (Ever-green)	Up to 3ft	Grown for foliage
Santolina	Cotton Lavender		1-2½ft	Grown for foliage
Senecio (Syn. Cineraria Martina)	Sea Ragwort, Dusty Miller	HA/P	1-1½ft	Grown for foliage
Stachys lanata	Lamb's Tongue, Lamb's Ear	P	1-1½ft	Grown for foliage

how to pick, prepare and arrange flowers

Which flower to pick

Never pick flowers which are in full bloom. Their petals will soon fall. The best ones to choose are those which are half open or just beginning to open.

When to pick

The best times to pick garden flowers are early morning or early evening, but never in the heat of the day. This is because at these times transpiration (plant language for sweating, when the excess water drawn from the soil is evaporated through the plant leaves) is lowest.

How to pick

Do not gather flowers without the aid of a good pair of secateurs or sharp flower scissors. Some stems are very tough and you can do a lot of damage pulling and tearing. Rough treatment gives the plant a severe shock, and may even partially uproot it.

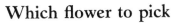

If you buy a bunch of flowers from a stall (far left) how can you use them to their best advantage? Short-stemmed Daisies look good put into a cup (above), and the vivid colours of Ranunculus are set off by a white mug (below).

Always cut the stems at an angle, so that they present the widest possible area to water. One of the few exceptions to this rule is the Lupin, which should be cut straight across.

If you are going to cut enough flowers to fill several different jugs and vases, it is a good idea to have a bucket of water in a shady place and put the flowers into this as they are picked. Many flowers, naturally enough, dislike being carried all around the garden and increasingly smothered by others.

All flowers and plants prefer rain water but if you do not possess a water butt, tap water which has been allowed to stand outside for a few hours to reach 'garden' temperature is nearly as good. At all costs avoid giving warm growing things an unpleasant shock by plunging them into icy cold water. In autumn or winter it may, therefore, be necessary to warm the water slightly.

Always leave freshly picked (or bought) flowers standing in deep water in a cool place for a few hours before you arrange them. If you pick them in the evening you can leave them overnight in a bucket to have a good drink.

Spring flowers benefit from standing for a few hours right up to their necks in water as this helps to stiffen their stems. Leaves and greenery, apart from those which have woolly leaves—for example, *Stachys Lanata* (Lamb's Ear)—like being totally submerged in water for a few hours before being arranged. *Gerbera* (Transvaal Daisy) and Tulips have a will of their own and tend to twist around or droop when arranged. Before giving them a long drink wrap their stems up to the heads in newspaper. This should stiffen the stems and encourage them to take up a fixed position. (There is no need to wrap each flower separately, but do not put more than six into one bunch.)

Prolonging their life

A little extra time and care can give your flowers a longer lease of life. Ideally, you should take precautionary measures before giving the flowers their long drink but, if this is not possible, make sure you do so before arranging them.

Leaves

Any leaves growing down stems which will be below water level should be stripped off. They take up space in the container or vase, and also make the water discoloured and smelly. This is true of most garden flowers, particularly *Brassicas* (the Cabbage family), Wallflowers and Stocks.

Hard woody stems

Plants like Lilac, Roses, Chrysanthemums and most flowering shrubs have hard woody stems. These should be hammered or split about half an inch up the stem.

Stems which bleed

The stems of flowers such as Poppies, Dahlias and *Euphorbia* (Spurge) which bleed or exude a white juice, benefit from being put for 10 to 30 seconds into two inches of boiling water. This treatment disperses the juice and helps them to drink. Protect the flower heads from the steam by wrapping them in a dishcloth. And if the stem ends look unhappy after this treatment do not worry and, above all, do not trim them off.

Sticky stems

Daffodils, Narcissi, and similar flowers exude a sticky substance. Hold the stem ends under warm running water to remove this, as it makes it difficult for them to drink.

Water

Always arrange flowers in tepid water. If you put a small piece of charcoal in the bottom of the container, the water will remain pure. Most flowers, with the exception of those such as Daffodils and Narcissi which exude a sticky substance, will last longer if you add sugar to the water (two teaspoons to one pint). Few flowers have a definite preference for a particular depth of water, but it is worth remembering those that do. Hellebore, for example, last better if they are arranged in deep water or floated in a bowl; Daffodils and Narcissi can last a very long time in a little water as long as they do not go dry; and Holly is best if it is not in water—leave it dry or arrange it in a plastic foam.

Flowers which travel

If you are cutting flowers which will be going on a journey, first put damp tissues or cotton wool around the stems, then newspaper and, finally, aluminium foil. This should ensure that they keep as fresh as possible.

Most flowers which have wilted in their travels can be revived if you recut the stems diagonally, place them up to their necks in a bucket of warm water to which sugar has been added (two teaspoons to one pint) and then leave them in a cool dark place for a couple of hours. Remember that all flowers, even if they travel no further than across the lawn, benefit from a long, undisturbed drink before being arranged.

Containers are vitally important. White with white always has a cool elegance (far right); Geraniums are set off by brass (top); Love-in-a-Mist and Roses have a classic simplicity that goes well with silver (centre), and orange containers echo the colour of Marigolds, and contrast with Marguerites (below).

Particular preferences

Certain flowers will last appreciably longer if you cater to their individual needs. Below are listed some tried and tested hints on how to deal with them.

Begonia and other hot-house plant leaves which are going to be used in an arrangement, should first be submerged for a few hours in water to which a spoonful of sugar has been added.

If you cut Broom when it is in flower, put the stems into very hot water for half a minute before arranging it.

Touch *Camellia* and *Gardenia* flowers only rarely, they bruise very easily.

Break Carnation stems between the joints if possible.

Put the ends of *Dahlia* stems in boiling water for 10 seconds. Avoid picking the larger blooms as they do not live long in water.

Delphiniums will last longer if you dip the tips of their stems in boiling water for 10 seconds, but even so the lower florets will probably still drop.

Delphiniums and Lupins benefit if their hollow stems are filled with water after they are cut, then plugged with cotton wool and left overnight in deep water.

Freesia lasts fairly well if the individual flower-heads are removed as soon as they die.

Cut *Hydrangea* on the new wood. Before arranging it place the stem ends in boiling water for a few seconds and then soak the flower-heads. *Hydrangea* absorbs water through the flower-head. Spray the flowers frequently to give a longer life in the vase.

Iris stems contain a lot of water which evaporates and causes the flower to droop. When gathered, each head should be wrapped in soft paper, and the flowers placed in deep water. Leave them in a cool place for an hour or more. This treatment hardens the stems and gives the flowers a longer life.

Cut off the dead heads of flowers such as *Irises* and Lupins to encourage the other buds to open.

Mimosa (also known as Wattle) lasts longer if it is sprayed twice a day.

Cut Peonies as soon as their petals begin to open and give them a long drink in deep warm water before arranging them.

Polyanthus (which are called Primrose in the United States) last better if you cut their stems short and arrange them in a massed posy.

If you char the stalks of Poppies over a flame before arranging them it will discourage them from fading.

Tulips only drink from the green part of their stems, so cut off any white portion at the bottom of the stem. Remember, too, that Tulips have one peculiar habit: if they can see themselves in a mirror they straighten up. This is useful if you are trying to get rid of a droop in their stems, but disconcerting if you have deliberately arranged them falling over a low container.

Violets last better if they are floated in tepid water for an hour or so before being arranged.

Wallflowers will die quickly if you cut them with long stems, so always cut their stems off short.

Large-headed varieties of *Zinnia* can have a wire pushed down the middle of the flower into the stem. This will stop the stem bending with the weight of the flower-head.

basic equipment

You can, of course, manage without all the equipment listed below. A bunch of Daisies will look attractive if you simply pop it into a pretty jug. And one or two Roses in a long narrow glass can look lovely. But it is worth collecting a certain amount of basic equipment so that you are well-prepared to tackle an important, somewhat more carefully thought-out, arrangement for a special occasion.

Flower scissors
These are invaluable and well worth their initial cost. Flower scissors are saw-edged and not only will they cope with the toughest stem in the garden but they also cut with ease through florists' wire and chicken wire.

Mesh or chicken wire
This is available from most florists' shops. The two inch mesh wire is best for most arrangements and buy the plastic-covered variety, if possible, as it does not rust. Cut it to approximately twice the width and twice the height of the container, then crumple it so that it stands above the top of the container in a central dome, leaving a few inches to fit securely over the edge of the container. Once fixed, it can be left permanently in place.

When you first encounter chicken wire it can be difficult to judge the exact amount needed and the extent to which it should be crumpled. Use too much and the flowers will not fit in; use too

little and it slips around in the container and gives an unstable arrangement. Aim at three layers of crumpled wire in all, with the holes evenly spaced.

Thin reel wire
You can get spools of this wire from most florists. (Or, alternatively, you could use thick fuse wire.) It can be

used to anchor the chicken wire around the rim of the container, or—as, for example, when the arrangement needs certain blooms to stand in a cluster—to bind together several flower stems. Do be careful not to strangle the flowers by binding the wire too tightly.

Florists' wire
This stiff, yet pliable, wire can be bought in 7-10 inch lengths. It is invaluable for wiring individual flowers.

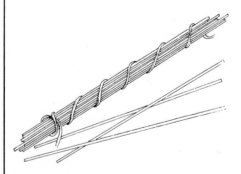

Pin-holders
A pin-holder is made up of a base with a lot of nail heads protruding from it. They can be bought in a variety of shapes and sizes, and sit in the bottom of the vase providing an anchor for heavy stems. It is worth securing the pin-holder to the bottom of the vase with plasticine to prevent it from shifting around and allowing your arrangement to topple over.

If by some misfortune you find you have flowers with stems too short for a particular container, fill the bottom of the container with sand or wet newspaper, sit the pin-holder on this false base and continue from there. The pin-holder makes it possible for the flowers to drink—direct contact with sand or newspaper might well prevent this.

Flower tubes

These elongated tubes or metal cones (which are sometimes known as water-pies) are useful for bringing individual flowers up to a required height in big formal arrangements for churches or receptions. The tube is fitted into the chicken wire, filled with water, and the flowers put into it. When the other flowers are arranged it should, of course, be invisible.

Plastic foam

A plastic substance (Oasis or Florapak, for example) is now often substituted for chicken wire, and is useful for a precious piece of silver which you do not want to scratch or stain. Line the container with aluminium foil and cut a piece of plastic foam to fit (it cuts with an ordinary kitchen knife). Soak the foam thoroughly before use. The flowers are inserted into it—if necessary, make holes for soft stems with a skewer —and absorb moisture from it. Remember, you still need to top up the arrangement with water.

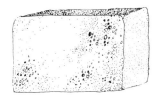

containers

Try not to think only in terms of 'vases', for there are few things which do not make pretty containers for flowers. Collect a variety of shapes, sizes and materials. The one thing to remember is that the base of the container must be in proportion to the top, otherwise your arrangement will be top-heavy and liable to fall over.

You can use every sort and shape of jug (blue and white, plain white, or white and gold china always seem to show off flowers well); old tea-pots; copper cooking pans; glasses of every shape and size; plain cylinders of white china; soup tureens; gravy boats, and blue glass chemists' jars. Heavy-based wine bottles and other bottles of good shape are also useful—provided the glass is a suitable colour. Even old egg cups can be used for miniature arrangements.

Tall cylinders in plain glass are good for Daffodils, Narcissi, Tulips and Poppies—the lovely stem shapes in the water are a great part of the charm of an arrangement. The glass must, of course, be kept sparkling clean. Any little water mark can generally be scrubbed away, or made to disappear by bleaching.

You need tall jars or jugs for large scale groups which stand on the floor—branches of flowering shrubs, or the tall dried subjects like Angelica, Artichokes and Teasels. Old cream and brown storage jars are excellent for this as they are heavy and not easily knocked over. Teapots are useful for Roses or annual mixtures, and tiny cups and glasses are ideal for individual posies to go on invalid trays, or to put by each table setting for a dinner party. Many feast-like meals have been ruined by the guests having to peer around a tall and splendid central arrangement, so keep the table decorations long and low, or put by each place a wine glass containing a posy, or a single gorgeous Peony or Rose.

Subdued colours like those of lovely old faded porcelain are best for flower containers. There is, of course, also a place for black pottery or matt metal, deep dark green and dark blue china and coloured glass (particularly green and blue). Care has to be taken that the container is not so bright and colourful that it dominates the flowers. It should be the perfect foil or background, or an equal partner echoing the colours of the flowers.

decorating with flowers

In the arrangement (above) David Hicks has exploited the rich creamy colour and wavy-edged petals of the roses. The leaves have been removed and the flowers crammed together in a bowl which is then placed inside a simple basket which enhances the colour of the roses.

Flower arrangements can be as vital to the style and decoration of a room as the curtains and cushions. If they are to add to a room and enhance its style, you need to do more than simply create a beautiful arrangement: the flowers and the arrangement need to be planned with the style and colour scheme of your room in mind.

Is the style in the room simple or dignified, austere or elaborate, modern or traditional? Is there a particular colour which the flower arrangement might pick up? Or some feature—alcove, mirror, fireplace, bookcase, polished table—which flowers could enhance or which would show them off to maximum advantage?

In a room of pale blue and white, for instance, hard yellow and red flowers would be out of place; while soft mauves and pinks, some deep purple or wine for contrast, and white or pale yellow flowers would be best; with silvery-grey foliage and in a silver container if possible. A room with a particularly beautiful carpet woven with Roses of vivid pinks and reds might be just right for abundant cut glass bowls of real Roses in equally vivid colours.

In a sparsely furnished room with a deliberately austere look, a massed arrangement would spoil the mood. A few flowers with some bare branches or just an arrangement of leaves in bold shapes (Hosta, Bergenia or Monstera) would be more appropriate, in a container of simple shape.

Against a dark-coloured wall, an all-white group could look particularly effective, especially if spot-lighted from above.

An old dresser might have its vertical lines emphasized decoratively by keeping on its shelves not just a row of plates, but a varied selection of small bowls, each with its own little Victorian-style posy.

A book-lined room needs flower arrangements in strong colours that will not be dominated by the massed book-bindings.

Flowers show up best if they stand

against plain, not patterned, curtains or walls, and with daylight or a lamp shining on them, not coming from behind. If you hold that one large flower arrangement is more effective than several small ones dotted about a room, it can be worthwhile to decide the best spot for this and then co-ordinate the background, an appropriate table or pedestal or other support, and the lighting so that the setting will be ready to receive a new arrangement each week. You will then know whenever you buy or pick flowers the precise setting into which they are to go.

If there is an over-busy pattern on the wallpaper, it is a good idea to keep a large brass or silver tray leaning against the wall behind the flowers or to site them against a mirror or piece of upright furniture.

In many rooms the mantlepiece is an obvious choice for flowers in summer or if modern heating has replaced the open fire. It carries the flowers at eye-level, and spread-out arrangements

are easier to accommodate there—particularly branches with blossom. There is also scope here for long, low arrangements instead of round bunches, for trailing effects with Ivy or Old Man's Beard falling gracefully over the edge of the mantlepiece, and for a double impact if a mirror hangs over the mantlepiece.

Wall-vases, too, are ideal for spreading or trailing effects at eye-level or higher. These can be bought or improvised with baskets or painted boxes hung on the wall, with a plastic pot inside them for water. With modern adhesives it is possible to fasten small containers onto tiles or low on a mirror. Such methods are useful when there is little room on furniture for flowers.

Flowers placed on large tables or other pieces of furniture may be associated with other ornaments such as china figures and pieces of silver or complementing the inlaid decoration in a marquetry surface. In such cases, both the base and the flowers should be

Graceful white tulips in a silver goblet. This arrangement is effective because of the simplicity of white flowers, green foliage and silver container. The classical shape and pure lines of the goblet complements the shapes of the tulips themselves.

chosen with these other features in mind, so that they will go well with their neighbours and neither clash nor dominate.

On a dining table, choice should be determined not only by the colour of the cloth or mats and the china but by some practical considerations: the need for people to see one another clearly across the table and not through a jungle, and for serving dishes to be passed unimpeded. One solution is to put a tiny bouquet in front of each place setting. Alternatively, a tall slender candelabrum might carry two or three posies above eye-level. For this arrangement, you need foil patty-pans secured with plasticine above the candle-holders and filled with water.

Foliage

A group of foliage in different shades of green or autumn tints can look very fresh and attractive.

White is extremely important, both for containers and flowers as it makes the most of all colours both vivid and subtle. But if you are using white alone be careful how much greenery you add—too much greenery can very easily dominate the flowers.

Silver-grey foliage is an essential ingredient in many arrangements as are the greeny-white flowers and the wonderful yellow-green of *Euphorbia*, which looks well with so many flowers.

Light

The amount and type of light your flowers will enjoy can be crucial. Blue and mauve flowers look lovely in strong sunlight or against a light wall—but they appear dull and grey-looking when put in a dark corner.

If you are arranging flowers for an occasion when they will be under electric light, always draw the curtains and put the light on while you are working. Electric light can do strange things to flower colours.

Again, if your flowers will stand on a sunny windowsill, then arrange them there—not on the kitchen table. Sunlight shining through flower stems can be very effective, but it can make an arrangement look straggly if you have not planned it.

Texture

Think about the texture of the flowers and leaves. A shiny leaf could be used with great effect to highlight a group of dull-surfaced leaves. And the texture of leaves always affects the weight and balance of an arrangement. Do not use strongly-textured leaves as outline material unless they are very pale in colour and, therefore, visually light, otherwise your flowers will look top-heavy.

The setting

Think about where you are going to put the flowers. Any flowers will look more attractive and give you greater satisfaction if you make sure that they are in proportion with the room, and the flowers in proportion both with the container and with each other.

Whenever possible arrange the flowers at the height at which they will be seen. If you cannot do this, say for example they are to go on a very high shelf, then crouch down from time to time to see how they will look from below. When the flowers will be seen from a distance —down a hall-way, or on a landing to

This is ideal for a dinner-party table

Frame a picture with a curved arrangement

The classic arrangement—a simple circle

A balanced triangle to set against a wall

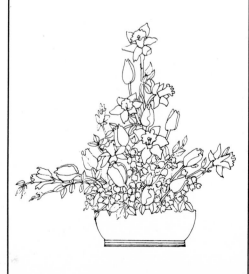

An asymmetric version of the triangle

For the modern home a modern arrangement

A narrow arrangement to fill an alcove

be seen from the foot of the stairs—walk away now and again and look back at them.

The background against which flowers will be seen is also important—it must not dominate too much. A too definite curtain or wallpaper pattern, for example, could make some flowers look faded and insignificant. And for table decorations make sure that table cloth or mats do not clash with the flowers. Always let the flowers be the important thing. Perhaps you might try white, or white and pink, flowers against a dark green wall; orange, yellow and white against grey in a rather cool room; green, mauve and purple against pale blue or white—the combinations and possibilities are endless.

Special occasions

If you are doing the flowers for a formal party, an anniversary, or some other special occasion you may well want a more formal arrangement.

Assuming that the chicken wire, pinholder, or foam is in place, and the container filled with tepid water, all you now have to do is arrange the flowers. Always have odd numbers of the different flowers, never an equal quantity. Try to have say five of one type and seven or nine of another. Take your time. Put the flowers in one by one and try the effect of each by holding it against the arrangement. Flowers object to being pushed into the chicken wire and then pulled out again when you decide they might look better elsewhere.

Despite the aura of mystery which surrounds the subject, the three basic steps to follow when attempting any arrangement are really extremely simple.

Outline

First put in the tall outline material—*Delphiniums*, *Gladioli*, *Forsythia*, Yew, Lime (with its leaves stripped off) or Grasses. Start by placing three pieces to fix the outline points, and then add a few more to complete the shape. All the stems should be aimed at the centre so that the finished arrangement flows from one point.

In a symmetrical arrangement an identical look to each side will give a stiff, flat appearance. Each flower should be slightly further back, and fractionally higher or lower than its opposite number.

Focal interest

The heavy, large blooms which are to form the focal point of the arrangement should be placed near the middle and fairly low. Important looking Peonies,

Rhododendrons, *Magnolias*, Roses, or tight clusters of berries, are ideal, but do avoid giving the effect of one central blob of colour. Choose flowers which will enhance but not totally dominate the arrangement.

Fillers

Intermediate 'filling' material—for example, Sweet Williams, Marguerites, or Sweet Peas—is used to tie in the heavy central flowers with the outline. Do not be tempted to fill in every single gap you can find. The effect of a flower arrangement can be ruined if it is too tightly packed. When in doubt, stop.

Church flowers

When arranging flowers in a church you must bear in mind the size, style and period of the church itself. Wild flowers will look delightful in the small chapel of an old Saxon or Norman country church, but could be totally out of place in a large church in a town or city. The same rule applies to the containers you use. Old-fashioned ones will look well in old churches and modern containers with their sharp definite lines look good in modern churches.

The flowers, particularly those arranged at the chancel steps, must be large and high enough to be visible and effective when seen from the back of the church, so exaggerate the arrangement a little and make it as high as possible. It is, too, often better to have flowers in all shades of one colour rather than lots of contrasting colours—the shape of the arrangement is then more easily appreciated from the back of the church.

Altar flowers present a difficulty because they often have to compete both with altar hangings and stained-glass windows. It is often a good idea to pick up one of the colours from the stained glass and carry this through to the flowers.

Always remember that the dim light, or electric light, found in churches may distort the colours of some flowers.

Care in container

Cut flowers are somewhat delicate beings. Even those which thrive in the most exposed corner of the garden develop invalid tendencies in the container. They all dislike draughts, full sunlight, gas fires, a dry overheated atmosphere, and being overcrowded. A light spray to keep up the humidity will be appreciated, and the container should be topped up with water—at room temperature not icy cold—every day. Cut flowers drink a surprising amount.

For the arrangement opposite, a round bowl was chosen to reflect the curved shape of the flowers.
To achieve this effect, soak florist's foam and put it into the bowl, moulding it into a domed shape. Cover foam with chicken wire and secure with silver florist's wire to hold the foam to the container. Cut all flowers with 2 inch stems and stick them into the foam to form a complete circle.

A charming country cottage style arrangement (above) in unsophisticated pinks and blues, with the bountiful look of a country garden. This section of flowers and foliage illustrates that, even with an abundance of wild and garden flowers to choose from, great care must be taken in selecting colours and shapes that will work together in an arrangement.

town house look

The average apartment or recently built house in a town tends to have small rooms and compact furniture—not much scope for outsize arrangements, nor a casual brimming-over look. Probably florists' flowers—few because of their cost—will be the material used. As for foliage, it is usually possible to find some on a country walk or in a friend's garden.

Even with such limitations, however, a distinctive style can be created, appropriate to the setting.

To make the most of limited space, use Snowdrops in miniature arrangements, or Lily-of-the Valley, Freesias, Ranunculus, Pinks and Crocuses and put these on a desk top, dressing table or hall window sill. Small urns are particularly suited to miniature arrangements, giving them extra importance.

Neat foliage in miniature arrangements can be provided by sprigs of Broccoli or Parsley, or leaves from a Peperomia plant. With delicately coloured flowers like Pinks, skeleton Magnolia leaves (from a florist or garden centre) could be used, sprayed white or silver. On a small dining table, such flowers could be wired into a long garland and laid (with candles) along the centre (or in a circle) just before the meal starts, having been kept in water meanwhile. Some flowers, because they remain tidy and do not sprawl, are well suited to a modern flat. Hyacinths for example, perhaps with some large Ivy leaves for contrast; massed Anemones or Marigolds cut short; Lilies with Laurel leaves and Solomon's Seal; Carnations, not with the over-used Asparagus Fern but among Holly leaves. A solitary branch or two of blossom, Eucalyptus, Pussy Willow or Chestnut buds may be all that is needed to make a corner of a room interesting, relying on linear composition to provide all the decoration that is needed. In autumn, *Symphoricarpus* (Snowberries) (white) and Pyracantha or Cotoneaster berries (red) add fresh interest; or use bare branches painted white.

Florists' flowers can be made more of, not only with cultivated foliage but with wild kinds brought home after a drive in the country. Add black Hypericum berries to a bowl of red Tulips, for instance, or even use a froth of *Chaerophyllum Sylvestre* (Cow Parsley) heads in a shallow dish on a coffee table, or an all-foliage group.

A very stylized effect can be created by buying a large ball or cone of flower arranging foam or making one of chicken wire (foam-filled) and entirely covering the surface with flower heads (Marguerites, Polyanthus or Anemones are a good choice). Such a ball of flowers can be hung up on a ribbon, or be placed on top of a short white rod held rigid in a flower pot of compost or sand. Cones of yellow Roses, Grapes and Ivy set on a pair of urns would be a handsome addition to a formal mantelpiece, and so would Redcurrants among white *Nicotiana* (Tobacco Plant).

country house look

If you live in town, you usually have to make do with bunches of one or two sorts of flowers and work with a limited palette of colour, texture and shape. But if you're fortunate enough to have a country garden, then you can build up a much richer mixture of blooms and buds, mixed with leafy herbs or flowering branches.

The country house way of arranging flowers is usually similar to the style for town house, with the same emphasis on carefully planned balance, the same types of vases and containers—altogether more studied than a cottage posy or the modern decorator's understated bunches.

For a formal room with large pieces of furniture (far right), a group of that most formal of flowers, the Lily. The white petals sparkle against the rich brown background colour and the young, delicate green of the fern adds freshness and life to an arrangement which might otherwise be rather lacking in vitality. This is an example of florists' flowers combined with country foliage.

Fragrant Lilies-of-the-Valley in a small basket — the bowl is concealed inside

A mixture of flowers in a small urn make an elegant arrangement

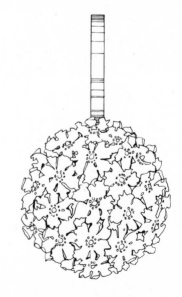

An anemone-covered ball of damp foam hung on a ribbon

Flowers arranged for special occasions could have a 'grander' look about them. Flowers from your garden—Escallonia, Roses and Single Pinks—can be combined into a delightful posy bowl (top left). Sprays of evergreen and autumn berries look elegant when arranged in a green glass container that shows their stem shapes (centre left).

Lime with its leaves stripped off, and Hosta Glauca leaves for a bold focal shape give an unusual touch to a somewhat more formal bowl (bottom left).

Bold, colourful country flowers—Peonies, Delphiniums and Stocks—can look marvellous together (right).

Below a step-by-step guide to flower arranging—first the outline material, then the focal interest and, finally, the fillers

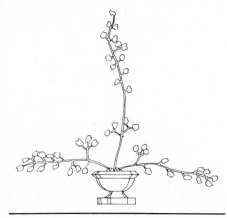

country cottage look

6

Even in town some homes manage to achieve a nostalgically countrified look —with simple pine furniture, oak chests and homespun curtains. In surroundings like these, formal flower arrangements would strike the wrong note. Cottage garden flowers are a good choice: Marguerites, Lupins, Delphiniums, Cornflowers, Honeysuckle, Anemones, Daffodils, Primroses, Marigolds, Pinks, Stocks, Nasturtiums and the like. Supplement these with wild flowers; and in autumn pick berries from the hedgerows: Bryony, Hawthorn, Elder, Rosehips and Blackberries still greeny-red, to use with trails of Ivy and Old Man's Beard. In spring, arrange Primroses or Crocuses among moss and ferns.

Containers should be in keeping— simple white pottery, an old blue and white patterned teapot, baskets (with a water pot or tin inside), a child's mug, even an old pair of scales. A shiny new galvanized bucket would have a certain splendour brimming with pink Peonies and mauve Lilac.

For the country cottage look, small arrangements look best as little rounded posies rather than in more contrived pyramids or asymetrical shapes. For large jugs or pots the aim should still be soft and artless, with the stems cut roughly the same length.

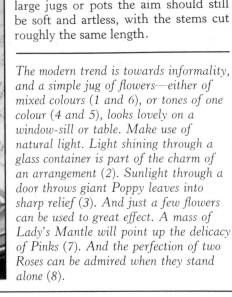

The modern trend is towards informality, and a simple jug of flowers—either of mixed colours (1 and 6), or tones of one colour (4 and 5), looks lovely on a window-sill or table. Make use of natural light. Light shining through a glass container is part of the charm of an arrangement (2). Sunlight through a door throws giant Poppy leaves into sharp relief (3). And just a few flowers can be used to great effect. A mass of Lady's Mantle will point up the delicacy of Pinks (7). And the perfection of two Roses can be admired when they stand alone (8).

7   8

the designer look

How do today's professional interior designers like David Hicks use flowers? Just as he collects interesting objects, chosen for their form and texture, and then places them very carefully in relation to the room as a whole, so does his choice and arrangement of flowers show equal care. Since he and many other modern designers are now returning to the use of pattern on carpets or curtains—often very bold, geometrical patterns suited to modern architecture—it is not surprising that in flower arrangement the 'interior designer' look is often one of great simplicity, with sometimes an almost stark handling of the flowers.

The emphasis is on the use of just one kind of flower in a container, not mixed bunches; and just one colour. The flowers are not 'arranged' in any obvious sense. They are, for instance, often plunged into a container so that only their heads show above it as a solid mass of colour. Again, in an utterly plain but big glass container, a mere half-dozen flowers may stand to one side, their stems clearly visible in the water, and forming a graceful part of the composition as a whole. (No wire or pin-holder is used.)

Preferred flowers are likely to be those with a simple, clearcut shape like Tulips, Water Lilies, Hostas or Arum Lilies or a bunch of *Cornus* (Dogwood). Preferred containers are equally simple and definite—straight cylinders, rectangles or cubes in steel, plain glass or undecorated china in a single strong colour. Flowers and container thus combine to make a single, emphatic statement.

An important 'colour' in interior design today is white, and often all-white flowers (without even their foliage showing) are massed in a coloured or neutral container for contrast. The container might, for instance, be a plain terracotta pot, a cylindrical black basket, varnished to shine in contrast with the white petals, or a green glass goblet of classic shape.

White walls may be used to show up the neat, symmetrical designs in a bunch of dried grasses and grains, their straw-like texture emphasized by the chromium tube in which they stand. Teazles and Globe Artichokes or a head of Giant Hogweed have geometric interest.

Kitchen jars in plain white pottery or in glass often provide the right effect as containers, but it is not difficult to improvise, by covering a cardboard box or tube with plain material (shiny black PVC, kitchen foil, pine-green felt—the choice is wide). and standing a jar out of sight inside it. Even a piece of drainpipe might be used, or a brass wastepaper bin.

With such very simple arrangements, lighting is particularly important. A spotlight wall-mounted or possibly shining up from the floor, is ideal, particularly if the flowers are on a glass table.

A beautiful and effortless-looking example of traditional flowers used in a modern way by David Hicks. Its beauty lies in the simplicity of the arrangement.

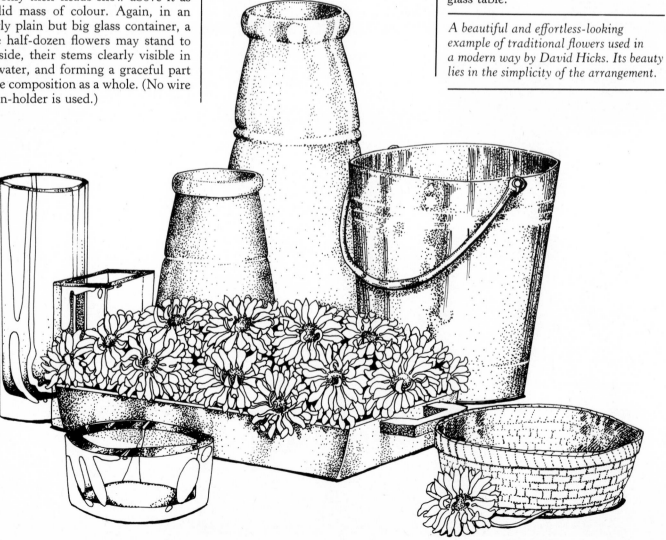

the period look

At different periods and in different countries, distinct styles of flower arrangement have emerged. The ancient Egyptians decorated rooms with cut flowers (mostly the Lotus, a Water Lily) and the Romans used festoons of Roses.

It can be fun to browse through art books of a particular period, or to do a little detective work in an art gallery, in order to spot, in paintings of interiors, just how the flowers used to be done—particularly if you have a room with furniture of a certain period.

Some really good films set in the past are executed with much care to get historical detail right: keep an eye open for the flower arrangements in them when you visit the cinema or watch television.

Flower varieties in Europe were few in medieval times; even such familiar ones as Daffodils, Tulips, Lilacs and Pinks had yet to be introduced. But a solitary white Lily in a pewter jug (from a 15th-century painting now in New York) and branches of Fir with colourful Lilies and Roses (painted by Raphael on a ceiling in Rome) are simple and appealing ideas. Voluptuous groups of rambler Roses in soft colours, in the style of Boucher (who decorated La Pompadour's boudoir) would strike the right note among rococo French furniture or Sèvres porcelain of the mid 18th century. Sprays of Cherry blossom might be placed on a piece of chinoiserie furniture, or beneath an old Japanese print hanging on the wall. Urns of fruit and Laurel leaves would enhance French Empire furniture. Chrysanthemums would look well in a room in which a fabric with a William Morris chrysanthemum pattern had been used for the curtains. Stylized Victorian posies might suit a mahogany table laid with Victorian cutlery. Huge Sunflowers could decorate a room in which there was a print of Van Gogh's Sunflower picture, Josiah Wedgwood (who even wrote a pamphlet on how to arrange flowers) designed urn-shaped vases specially for them. Filled with graceful and loosely composed arrangements, these complement the Chippendale or Sheraton furniture of Wedgwood's own time.

For a twenties look, use a simple and very plain curve of flowers in a geometric container of rough pottery or thick glass.

Dutch painter look

Perhaps most striking of all period styles was the late 17th century Dutch style. There was then a fashion amongst Dutch painters like Van Huysum for huge pictures of mixed flowers, in a free and spontaneous conglomeration which has a very exuberant look. The whole effect is of a great mass, rich in colour and variety—a deep and rather open arrangement always slightly disarranged. Outsize Roses, Peonies and Tulips feature prominently. Strangely, the Dutch who liked these flower arrangement pictures did not then go in for real flower arrangements in their homes.

Achieving this look of abundance depends upon several necessities: plenty of space for its display, a big container, and huge quantities of flowers. If you do not have a bottomless pocket, a brimming garden (supplemented by hedgerow flowers and plants) is essential.

Easier (and cheaper) to copy is the Tudor custom of a small nosegay of herbs and scented flowers in every bedroom. This was believed to be healthy and is certainly a pleasure at bedtime—especially in a guest's room.

The graceful and studied arrangement (right) reflects the lines and glowing colours of a 17th century Dutch still life painting.
The rich 'painting' effect, achieved by a careful choice of colours and the use of trails of blackberry and vivid hips, haws and butterflies, can be used as an outstanding decorating feature to enhance a room or hallway.
The container — a deep bowl — was chosen for its simple shape and rich colour.
To prepare the arrangement, split all the wood stems and split and hammer the gentian stems.
Soak a block of florist's foam for about fifteen minutes, cut it in half and place in the bowl. Cover the top of the foam with fifteen gauge chicken wire. Wire this base to the container with silver florist wire to prevent the arrangement slipping about when you are working on it. Make a reversed 'L' shape with the hips, haws and blackberries. Next, add the foliage and finally the flowers.

the oriental look - ikebana

Many of our well-known flowers came originally from the East (and some of our best known designs of china vases too). In China, the art of flower arranging was an important part of life, and of religion. Extremely simple in appearance, each flower arrangement was intended to present the viewer with just one or two beautiful objects to contemplate completely (a mass of flowers was felt to be spiritually indigestible), and each flower was considered to be a perfect microcosm of all life. Further, Buddhists believe all life, including plant life, is sacred, and that to squander cut flowers is wrong. Modern ecologists would sympathize with this view (and so would anyone who finds the price of florists' flowers rather daunting, in the winter particularly).

Ikebana, the Japanese style, is still taken very seriously, with 'grand masters' teaching it in special colleges. A lot of religious symbolism is involved, as well as strict rules about adhering to nature's ways. For instance, a flower must never be placed higher than a tree branch nor a mountain plant lower than a field one. And no one should do a flower arrangement while tense or depressed, the experts say.

To be really skilled in Ikebana, you need to attend a course. But even without doing so the general look of oriental flower arrangement can be appreciated and to some extent reinterpreted for the home.

There are few limits to the kind of flowers which can be used for Ikebana, but here are some very characteristic combinations: Pine branches with Camellias, Azalea branches with white Chrysanthemums, Hosta leaves with Peony heads, Easter Lilies with Pussy Willow, Cherry blossom boughs with Monstera leaves, Irises with Water Lilies.

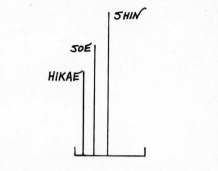

Main stems for Moribana (medium size)

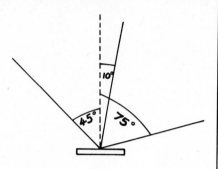

Main stems at angles to the vertical

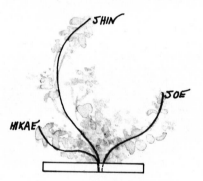

Main stems in Moribana Risshin-Kei No.1 Oyo (example by Stella Coe opposite)

For Ikebana you will need two kinds of containers — a shallow, horizontal bowl for Moribana style and a tall vase for Nageire style. The three main stems in Moribana and Nageire arrangements are generally known as Heaven (Shin), Man (Soe), and Earth (Hikae or Tai). The Shin is the longest and most prominent line, Soe is the medium and Hikae the shortest line. Additional branches or flowers (jushi) are added only after these three have been placed. The pin holder or Kenzan (which must always be covered) is usually placed asymmetrically and the numbers of branches are deliberately used in odd numbers to avoid the predictability of symmetry. In the same way the jushi are of varying lengths, always shorter than the main stem. The length of the main stems depend on the size of the container. For a small arrangement the Shin is the size of the width and depth of the container, Soe is three quarters of the Shin and,

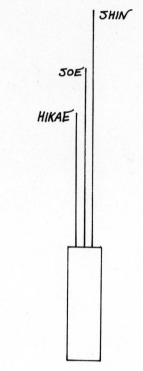

Main stems for Nageire (Medium size)

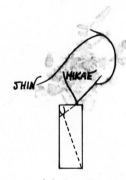

Main stems in Modern Free Style Nageire (example arranged by Stella Coe overleaf)

Hikae is three quarters of Soe. For a medium arrangement the Shin is the size of the width of the container plus the depth and up to half as much again. Soe is three quarters of Shin. Hikae is three quarters of Soe. In a large arrangement the Shin is twice the size of the width of the container plus the depth. Soe is three quarters of Shin and Hikae is one half of Soe. These measurements apply to both Moribana and Nageire arrangements — except that in Nageire the measurements are for the length of the stems above the rim of the container.

Basically the three main stems are placed at certain angles. These angles are measured from an imaginary vertical line coming from the place when the Shin branch is put in the Kenzan. The tips of the main branches should be at 10°, 45° or 75° from the upright zero. As long as the tips of the branches maintain the angle they can be in any direction on the plane.

*Example of Moribana No1 Oyo
arranged by Stella Coe*

An example of an Ikebana arrangement—
Nageire Modern Free Style by Stella Coe

An arrangement of flowers and foliage
reflecting the influence of Japanese
flower arranging style — note the way
in which an unusual container is used

eye-catching table centres

Low centrepiece of crisp green parsley surrounding bright radishes

A bowl of fruit can hardly ever look dull, but with a little imagination it can be made into a really eye-catching decoration for a table, sideboard or buffet, particularly if there is no flower arrangement in the room. Alternatively, flowers and fruit may be combined in one arrangement, perhaps with walnuts and almonds sprayed gold or bronze. Some vegetables are so decorative that they, too, can join in the fun: Globe Artichokes, Broccoli and Corn Cobs for their interesting shapes; Tomatoes, Aubergines, Pimentos and Parsley for their brilliant colours.

Particularly decorative fruits, usually confined to serving dishes are worth displaying, include Lemons (wired if necessary), home-grown Strawberries, still on their long stems, and clusters of Redcurrants.

Bunches of Grapes, black or green, and trailing Cherries are now almost a cliché added to large flower arrangements but they are undeniably handsome. For really outsize groups in the style of the Dutch masters, halved Water Melons and Red Cabbages or whole Pineapples can add a crowning splendour.

Particularly appropriate to add to a bunch of autumn flowers would be a branch or two from a Plum tree with fruit on; or some Lemons among white *Narcissi* and green leaves in spring. Conversely, foliage plants can be used to transform a bowl of fruit—small-leaved Ivy trailing down or crowns of *Chlorophytum* springing out among the fruit, for example. A soaked piece of plastic foam, foil-wrapped, will supply them with water, or any tiny container such as a pill tube.

For a really extravagant effect on a special occasion, a high cone of flowers, nuts and fruit in contrasting shapes (Apples, Bananas, Grapes—even a Garlic), together with evergreens or dried leaves, could be entirely sprayed in gold—spectacular if stood on a shocking-pink cloth. Start with a tall cone of crumpled chicken wire or plastic foam as a base, wedged firmly into a sturdy container which should also be sprayed gold. A more subtle effect could be achieved with a silver spray, and a delicate pink cloth, mauve candles and gauzy ribbons.

A silvery sparkle which does not spoil fruit for eating can be achieved by dipping Grapes (or berries) in beaten egg white and then into caster sugar, and leaving to dry.

A Pineapple is in itself a resplendent object, but it can also be the basis of a colourful buffet table decoration. First slice it ready to serve, then reassemble it as if uncut, making sure each slice goes back into its original position. Then, with the help of cocktail sticks and florist's wires, make a dazzling array of silver and red flowers among the leaves at the top (which might first be sprayed silver), using kitchen foil petals with glacé cherry centres.

For simpler or more natural effects, build a small still life on a flat wooden platter (such as a cheeseboard), a bamboo mat or a very shallow basket. A few Apples and Oranges, some Nuts, Parsley or Celery tops for foliage and a single Chrysanthemum head—these everyday things can combine into a pretty centrepiece for a table. Alternatively, make a low group of Tomatoes and Lemons, some baby Carrots (well scrubbed), Lady's Fingers or Courgettes and Radishes with a few yellow Chrysanthemums (concealing their water pot). These fruit and vegetable arrangements are handy in winter when flowers are scarce and expensive. The same materials could also be used in a tall arrangement. Three plates (large, medium and small) can be raised in tiers on which to arrange the vegetables with the help of two food cans in between. Foliage that will trail over the edges and downward is a desirable addition. 'Cabbage leaf' dishes are another natural choice for fruit and vegetable arrangements.

Cocktail sticks or skewers are often helpful in mooring fruit or vegetables in place, and cooking oil can be used for polishing Ivy leaves, Walnuts and Courgettes, for example.

Cabbage, radishes and artichoke heads as a table centre (opposite) on a green cloth. The flowers in the jugs reflect the vegetable colours

A high cone of apples, bananas, grapes and foliage for a side-table

Dimpled strawberries and shiny round currants with contrasting green foliage

leaves and berries

Decorative leaves and berries can be as effective as flowers in arrangements, and can make a surprisingly attractive display (see opposite).

Leaves

For an interesting arrangement of foliage you will need contrasting forms and colours—leaves of flowers such as Peonies, the large heart-shaped leaves of Bergenia, tall, slender Iris, and ornamental Vine, the leaves of which turn crimson, pink or orange in the autumn.

Hostas, with their big, ribbed leaves, are always useful in arrangements, *Hosta glauca* has large grey-green leaves and another variety has white margins around the leaves. Mahonia, with its holly-like leaves, also provides useful foliage with evergreen leaves and bluish-black clusters of berries. *Euonymous* (Spindle Tree) has varieties with green, gold and white leaves with bright pink or red berries and autumnal foliage.

Trees provide basic material throughout the year, giving the fragile green of spring and the rich red and yellow colourings of autumn to contrast with the deep tones of evergreens. In winter the hips of Wild Roses are available, and so are the fruits of many hardy ornamental shrubs.

Herbs

Herbs should never be overlooked for their use in arrangements, with or without flowers. Their charm lies not only in the subtle shades of green but in the delicate perfume of the fresh herbs. Silver Sage and Rosemary, Bay stems with their dark, shiny leaves and Lavender are delightful.

Berries

Decorative berries include the scarlet berries of *Crataegus corallina*, all the Berberis have luscious bunches of berries, ranging from orange, yellow and purple to the translucent pinky-white berries of *Berberis jamesiana*. The *Pyracantha* species, Firethorns, produce enormous quantities of yellow, orange or scarlet berries. Also useful in foliage arrangements are the feathery seed heads of Clematis and the metallic blue heads and silvery stems of *Echinops banaticus* (Globe thistle); *Physalis franchetii* (Chinese lanterns or Cape Gooseberries) with their inflated orange-red calyx; *Cornus alba 'Sibirica'* (Red-barked Dogwood) with its brilliant crimson shiny spiky stems; *Cotoneaster* and the big yellow or crimson clusters of *Sorbus* (Mountain Ash).

Fruits

Other things to use in these kinds of arrangements include Horse Chestnuts, enclosed in their thick spiky protective cases and twigs of Oak with the acorns still attached. Gather these before they fall from their cups. Catkins last for several weeks in the home. *Salix* (Willow) in its many varieties produces long gold or silvery tassels in very early spring, and so does the Hazel and Alder.

Preserving leaves and berries

The leaves of various trees and shrubs can be preserved with glycerine. To do this, bruise the stems at the base and place them in a mixture of one part of glycerine to two parts of water. After about three weeks the stems will absorb sufficient liquid to preserve the leaves in varying shades of bronze and brown. This should be done before the end of the summer while the leaves are still fresh, as they lose their power of absorption in the autumn. Oak, Magnolia and young Eucalyptus are particularly suitable for this treatment.

Berries can be preserved by brushing them with a mixture of $\frac{1}{2}$ clear shellac and $\frac{1}{2}$ alcohol. Hang them up to dry in an airy place.

The simplest way of skeletonizing leaves is to immerse them in water for several weeks until the leaf tissues can be gently rubbed off the vein structure. Do not change the water as this slows up the decomposition. Another way is to boil the leaves very slowly in detergent to soften the tissues and then remove the pulp carefully with a knife.

Whichever method you use, the skeletons can then be soaked in ordinary household bleach solution to remove the colour. Take care not to leave the skeletons in the solution too long as the bleach will eventually make the leaves disintegrate. Dry the leaves gently and either press flat between two sheets of blotting paper or allow to curl.

Leaves, fruits and berries for decoration

Fern shaped leaves
Sanguisorba — fresh green
Senecio — greyish white
Filipendula — green shades
Thalictrum — shiny green

Rush shaped leaves
Crinium — light green
Galtonia — dull bluish green
Tradescantia virginiana — dull green

Heart shaped leaves
Bergenia — green in spring, crimson in winter
Macleaya — green, white underneath
Doronicum — light green
Crambe — greyish green

Berries and fruits
Celastrus orbiculatus — orange 'pods' with scarlet seeds
Viburnum — evergreen varieties — red, blue and black, sometimes translucent berries
Sorbus — varieties have fruits ranging from white, creamy yellow, pink and white to bright red
Skimmia japonica — scarlet berries
Cotoneaster — different varieties produce yellow, red or scarlet berries
Arbutus — fruits similar to small pendulous strawberries
Ilex — typical form has scarlet red berries in large clusters

Shrubs for coloured autumn foliage
Azalea — deciduous varieties
Acer
Amelanchier
Cotinus
Rhus
Viburnums — opulus varieties

Shrubs with scented foliage
Lavender
Myrtle
Eucalyptus
Cistus
Sweet Bay
Rosemary

dried flowers and leaves

Flowers grown especially for drying for interior decoration are called 'Everlastings' or the lovely French name 'Immortelles' and are generally hardy or half-hardy annuals. They are well worth growing as they are attractive and last well in borders, and when dried their daisy faces stay bright and summery-looking throughout the winter.

There are endless variations on what to do with dried flowers—from formal little Victorian posies of *Helipterum* (Immortelles) and Wheat and Grasses, huge containers of the giants like Angelica, Teasel, *Heracleum* (Cow Parsnip) and Artichoke, throwing wonderful shadows on a plain white wall. Simply arrange them as you would fresh flowers—but without water of course. If you are putting the flowers into a lightweight container it is a good idea to put dry sand or gravel in the bottom of the container to give weight and stability to the arrangement.

The easiest way to dry flowers is simply to tie them into bunches and hang them up in a dry, cool, airy place (below).

Dried flowers should not look dreary. Put dried foliage and autumn berries with your dried grasses (right).

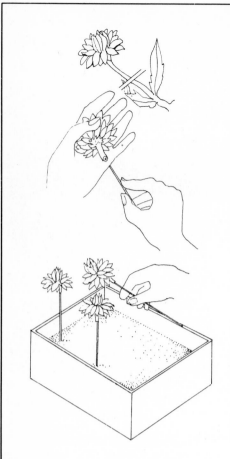

Wired flowers are dried standing in sand

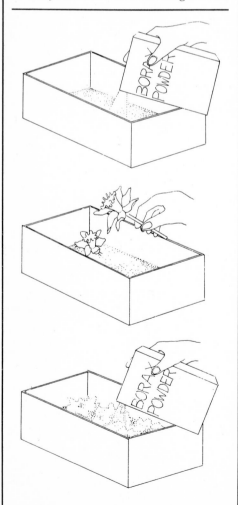

Borax can be used to dry flowers easily

Fresh flowers can be successfully added to an arrangement of dried flowers if you are careful about matching the texture and feel of the two types. Either put the fresh flowers into a small container and put this into a bigger one containing the dried flowers or, for individual fresh flowers, use crumpled chicken wire in the dried arrangement and thrust tubes into this to take the fresh flowers.

Do beware of treating a dried flower arrangement as a fixture. Rearrange it every few weeks, add or subtract something, or move it to another place—few things look sadder or more depressing than a dusty group of dried flowers that has been sitting in the same place for months.

One note of warning—candles and dried flowers do not mix. Any dried flowers placed near lighted candles will probably catch fire.

Dried flowers, of course, need not be put into containers. Experiment with them—the possibilities are boundless. Various trees, posies, and table decorations can be made with dried flowers pushed into Styrofoam, or a similar substance. Small indoor hanging baskets can be filled with dried flowers instead of pot plants. Hanging ornaments can be made using a ball of Styrofoam or plasticine tied around with ribbon to hang it up by, and filled in with dried flowers. If some of them have fragile stems and prove difficult to insert, pin them in place through the flower-head.

Planting flowers for drying

As with every sort of annual sowing, the ground should have been well prepared the preceeding autumn or winter—dug over, stones and weeds removed, forked and raked flat—before sowing the seeds in spring.

Sow the seeds either in groups or in rows when the soil is fairly dry and then thin out the seedlings to 3-6 inches apart (about three-quarters of the final expected height of the plant). Alternatively, seeds can be sown in boxes under glass, pricked out into good potting compost about 30 to 35 to a box, and planted out when there is no longer any danger of frost.

Picking

Keep an eye on the flowers during the summer to be sure of cutting them at the right moment on a day when they are not at all damp. Do not let the flowers open fully or begin to set seed or you will get showers of fluff when you hang them up to dry. With the larger branching types like *Helichrysum*, when the main flower has been picked, you get many smaller ones all down the stem a few weeks later. Pinching out the growing point before you pick flowers will have the same effect but give you larger secondary flowers.

Drying

When the flowers are picked, strip any leaves from the stems, tie them in small bunches or bundles and hang them upside down to dry. If the bunches are too large the stems may tangle or be damaged. Flowers dried in a light position become brittle and lose some of their colour, and flowers become mildewed in the damp—a shed or garage may be dry in summer but it could be too damp in autumn to dry flowers in. Ideally, hang the flowers in a cool, dry, airy, shady place.

If the stems are very short (or, like those of *Helichrysum Bracteatum*, look somewhat ugly when dried) cut the stem one inch from the head, push a length of 20 gauge florists' wire (or a finer gauge if the flowers are small) up the stem into the flower-head and push the wires into sand or dry plastic foam. Leave the flowers to dry in this position. As they do so the wire will rust into place.

If you are just beginning to experiment with dried flowers start by drying the brightly coloured varieties—the purples, yellows and golds—as these are less likely to lose any of their colour during the drying process.

An alternative method of drying flowers which is somewhat more complicated involves the use of a desiccant such as borax powder, available from chemists. But it is worth taking the extra trouble as this is often a more successful way of drying flowers which are not true everlastings.

Cover the bottom of a box with the borax powder, carefully lay the flowers in this, and then pour in more powder until the flowers are completely covered—taking care that it runs in between all the petals and stamens. Then simply leave them. The borax powder draws all the moisture from the flower. (An older and cheaper alternative to borax is sand—but it is often too heavy and damages the flowers.)

Inspecting the flowers to see if they are dry is a delicate operation as you must be careful not to damage them as you uncover them. The length of time it will take to dry the flowers obviously varies, but it is more often a matter of hours than days. Small Roses and Pansies, for example, need only about 12 hours and Cornflowers 36 hours.

True everlastings

True Everlastings or Immortelles are those flowers grown specifically to be dried. They are annuals and grow best in a sunny place.

Acroclinium Roseum syn. Helipterum Roseum is a well-known Straw Daisy with petals softer than those of its near relative *Helichrysum Bracteatum*. It grows to about 2 feet tall and has daisy-like pink or white flowers of papery texture. In a good summer it should flower six weeks after it has been sown, so you can grow and dry it in the same year.

Ammobium Alatum Grandiflorum (Everlasting Sand Flower) has silvery-white petals and a domed yellow centre. It does grow to 2 feet tall but its stems are short in proportion to its flower-heads and you may need to lengthen them when you come to arrange them.

Gomphrena Globosa (Globe Aramanth or Batchelor's Buttons) was a favourite in Elizabethan gardens. It grows 12-18 inches high, has white, red or purple globular flowers and is a half-hardy annual.

Perhaps the best known of all the everlastings is *Helichrysum Bracteatum* (the Straw Flower) which include both 3-4 feet tall and shorter dwarf varieties. It has flowers rather like those of a stiff, shiny-petalled double daisy in an assortment of colours—orange, wine-red, apricot, yellow, gold and white. The flowers should be picked as soon as they begin to open. Do not wait until they are in full bloom.

Helipterum Manglesii, also known as *Rhondanthe Manglesii*, grows 12-18 inches tall and has tiny daisy flowers in clusters of florets—white, pink, or rose; both double and single blooms.

Statice (Limonium) Sinuatum (Sea Lavender) grows 1-2 feet high and has papery flowers in blue, mauve, or white. Its perennial cousins are *Statice (Limonium) Latifolium* which has mauve flowers—this is somewhat taller, reaching 2-3 feet—and *Limonium Bonduellii* which has yellow flowers and grows to 1-2 feet. Both of these are equally good for drying.

Xeranthemum is another everlasting with silvery pink, mauve or white flowers. It grows to 2 feet tall and must be sown where it is to flower as it resents being moved.

Helipterum Roseum—a pink or white Daisy

Ammobium Alatum—silver-white and yellow

Gomphrena Globosa—red, white or purple

The many-coloured Helichrysum Bracteatum

White, pink or rose Helipterum Manglesii

Sea Lavender—white, mauve or blue

Xeranthemum—silver-pink, mauve or white

A mass of dried grasses and flowers in subtle shades of brown and beige is used to great effect in a daring mixture of antique and modern (left).

An arrangement of grasses and seed heads is given touches of brilliant orange by the inclusion of some dried Cape Gooseberries (right).

An enchanting country bowl full of dried grasses, seedheads, Everlastings and a spray of Honesty pods (below).

About wild flowers

The fragile beauty of a group of flowers growing wild in a field, along the side of a road, or on derelict ground in the middle of a city, can sometimes be more eye-catching than the most well-tended garden border—because they are, as it were, an unexpected bonus. People who usually have no desire to pick garden flowers often pick wild ones, and bemoan the fact that they do not live long in the vase.

Learning about wild flowers is a rewarding experience in itself, particularly if you discover a species which was feared to be extinct in your area. Modern agricultural methods and insecticides are, sadly, killing off some wild flowers, although one recent encouraging discovery in England was that rare specimens of wild flowers are now flourishing on the protected banks of motorways. Incidentally, the more you can learn about wild flowers the greater your knowledge of cultivated flowers will be, for they are all related.

Wild flowers, unfortunately, never last as long when picked as cultivated flowers—but given care they last long enough, and surely their ephemeral quality is part of their charm. To ensure the longest possible life for them, only pick flowers which look mature and healthy. Give them the usual treatment for travelling (see page 20) and when you get home steep them up to their necks in water for at least three hours, or overnight if possible, and then arrange them. Give them plenty of water—they drink a surprising amount.

Many wild flowers are so attractive that they really are worth picking to enjoy just a for a few hours. What could be nicer for a children's summer party than a large blue and white jug cascading with Buttercups on a gingham cloth, and who cares if they drop the next day? Do not, however, pick a bunch of Dandelions and put them on a table as a centre-piece for an informal dinner party. While you are in the kitchen basting the joint, those glorious golden heads will close with the setting sun!

Wild flowers that last

Queen Anne's Lace or Cow or Hedge Parsley does last very well in water, as do its cousins in the family *Umbelliferae* (Carrot and Parsnip flowers, Fennel and Angelica) which should last over a week in water. And wild Daisies, like all members of the *Compositae* family (Michaelmas Daisies and Chrysanthemums), last longer—up to two weeks.

Grasses have the longest life of all. And a jar or jug of tall wild grasses with an ear or two of Wheat or Barley (taken from the edge of a field after harvesting) make a graceful, feathery arrangement.

Why not plant your own?

If you have no opportunity to pick flowers wild in the spring, then why not plant a little group of Primroses, Violets, Scyllas and Aconites in a corner of the garden? Then you can pick and enjoy your own 'wild' flowers.

Pressing wild flowers

One of the greatest pleasures of being in a country environment is to go out and pick a bunch of wild flowers, put them in a jug to decorate the dining table, identify them and, finally, press them, preserving their beauty for ever. There is a book of pressed flowers in a library in Oxford, England which were picked and pressed in the fourteenth century. The colours are still bright while the flowers themselves have been dead for six hundred years.

To press the flowers either put them individually between blotting paper or tissues between the leaves of a heavy book or in the middle of a pile of magazines, or use a flower press if you have one. The flowers should be dry within two or three weeks, unless their heads are very thick.

This fascinating and rewarding passtime need not be confined to wild flowers. Marigolds, Pansies, *Anchusa* and *Verbascum*, Nasturtium and *Delphinium*, Geranium and *Clematis*, Hellebore and *Euphorbia* can all be effectively pressed.

Using pressed and dried flowers

Anything that can be done with pressed flowers can be done with dried ones, too. And sometimes more successfully, as dried flowers need not be flat—you could, for example, build up three-dimensional flower pictures—but can be pressed flat if necessary for say, table mats.

Collage pictures made up of pressed or dried flowers are very attractive, and whereas a book of pressed flowers may be put away and forgotten, a picture is a permanent reminder of a holiday or weekend.

· Choose a backing material which will

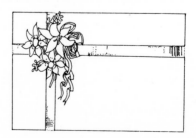

harmonize with the flowers—plain or coloured paper, linen, silk, hessian—and mount it on a backing board. To fix the flowers to the backing dab a very little latex adhesive onto the back of the flower—if you use too much adhesive it will soak through and discolour the flower-head—then gently put the flower into place in the collage. Use a soft paint-brush or a pair of tweezers to lift flower petals.

If you want to protect your finished picture with glass remember to fix a beading behind the frame to lift the glass so that it does not flatten the flowers.

Attractive **door finger plates** can be made by cutting white cardboard to the size of a perspex finger plate, sticking pressed flowers to the card and then covering this with the perspex.

Table mats can be similarly made. Use a backing of felt and a top surface of perspex, or glass cut to size by a glazier, of a thickness recommended to resist heat. Seal the edges of the mats with a strong adhesive tape.

Glazed screens or windows, matchbox tops, and even book covers can all be decorated with pressed or dried flowers. And when wrapping presents you could give them an original finishing touch by adding small garlands or sprays of dried flowers or pressed leaves.

A collage of dried wild flowers and plants is easy to make and brings a breath of country air into a town home. The flowers are stuck with a little multi-purpose glue to a board; glass is mounted over them and framed. Butterflies give extra charm—you can catch them yourself or, more easily, buy them from a dealer.

You can fill a tiny basket with dried flowers, or make dried flower trees for decoration (above).

These trees are simple to make. Cut your basic shape, using Styrofoam or a similar substance, put in flowers to give the outline to the tree, then simply fill in with dried flowers. You could, of course, substitute cones, and seed heads for flowers (see diagrams on the right).

There are many novel and decorative ways of using dried flowers. You can bind them into posies, decorate Chinese soup spoons or bowls with flowers, make hanging balls of dried flowers or make a dried flower candle base—but be careful not to let the candle burn down too far (above).

Dried flowers dyed brilliant colours are eye-catching but you usually have to buy them ready-dyed (left).

arrangements for seed heads and dried materials

The variety of shapes to be found in seed heads when autumn comes is, if anything, even greater than those of flowers, more than making up for any lack of colour. Strange, beautiful and dissimilar, seed heads can be combined in decorative groups that will outlast cut flowers or pot plants, survive even the worst effects of central heating or air conditioning and can cost nothing.

Just consider the wealth of material there for the taking. Delicate Cow Parsley 'umbrellas', the silver pennies of Honesty, big Corn cobs and the strange papery leaves surrounding them, stems of grain like Barley or Oats, Larch and Pine cones, lacy Love-in-a-Mist with its little balloons, neat seed spires from the *Hosta* (Plantain Lily), sprays of dry and yellowy *Alchemilla mollis*, round Poppy heads, tall shafts of Hollyhock or Delphinium, Japanese Lanterns, bobbles from Plane trees, winged Sycamore seeds in bunches, globes of Onion seed heads, Beechnuts, the dry white bells left after Bluebells have flowered, rusty spikes of Sorrel or Dock, all kinds of nuts, Bullrushes, orange berries from Irises and red ones from Peonies, spiky teazles, and many more from the garden or hedgerows. Collecting while on holiday is a pleasant way to pass the time and can provide materials to make a very individual souvenir. Small arrangements of dried seed heads make excellent presents.

One way to mount a holiday trophy in permanent form is on a wall panel, fastening the seed heads on a board with glue and small strips of plastic sticky tape (the kind used for insulation or to mend plastic items). If the seed heads are carefully arranged, the fixtures will not show. Combine the seed heads with dried leaves and flowers, interesting pieces of bark, dried fungus and lichen, even seashore finds like shells and dried seaweeds. As the first step, insert a screw or hook in the top of the board by which to hang it on the wall: this is difficult to do after the seed heads have been fastened down. Next year, from a holiday in some quite different place, you could make a companion piece of the same size but with a very different assortment of holiday finds evoking the distinctive scenery of the

place. Another way to make a wall panel, large or small, is to find a lid of suitable size, round or square, line it with a sheet of polythene (plastic bags will do) and pour into it a layer, ½-1 inch thick, of Polyfilla powder mixed with just enough water to make it spreadable. Press a loop of strong wire for hanging into the top edge before arranging the seed heads on the wet paste. First arrange them on the table in the way you want. Once they have been put on the paste they should not be shifted about. Leave overnight, and when the panel has set, it can be lifted out, for it does not stick to the polythene.

For a small wall plaque, a block of florist's plastic foam wrapped in foil could be glued to a wicker dish or table mat and the stems pushed into this. If you want to make a still life of seed heads or other materials to stand on a table or mantlepiece, a large lump of clay or other modelling material can be the basis for it. While it is still soft push in the seed heads until the surface is completely hidden by the arrangement. Semi-perishable materials such as berries or evergreens can go in too, though they will not last long.

You could aim for a look of abundance and variety or make a composition from only two or three items. Or take a specific plant or tree and concentrate on it for example, acorns, dried Oak leaves, and Oak apples grouped on a small Oak log.

Alternatively, simply compose the materials as you would in flower arrangement, using chicken wire or plastic foam, but without any water. Copper and brass containers, earth-coloured pots, wooden bowls and baskets suit this sort of material, rather than glass, china or silver.

A wire plant basket could be the basis for a hanging arrangement.

Cones and many other seed heads can, with the help of a twist of wire, be mounted on dried stems or slender twigs before joining a group. Dried seed heads need no treatment before use, but those with a tendency to disintegrate, such as bullrushes, will last longer if sprayed with hair lacquer. Most seed heads lack colour, but russet ones are not hard to find and some are bright yellow. For a Christmas

arrangement, either of these colours would show up well if provided with some artificial snow (detergent sprinkled around or mixed to a paste with a little water) and a few evergreens or Ivy kept fresh in a pot of water tucked out of sight.

Add a few silver or gold glass baubles if you like.

If you want a vivid splash of colour among the natural tones of the seed heads, some could be dipped into dye or a pot of poster paint, sprayed with gold, or sprinkled with glitter which will stick if varnish is sprayed over first. But do not overdo these things. Beechnut husks are particularly pretty painted bright red inside with the outside left natural, and wired to twigs as if they were flowers.

Combine dried material with everlasting flowers or artificial decorations—for instance, silvery Honesty mingled with turquoise paper butterflies glued to a few fine stems; a heap of Pine cones mixed with frankly fake red Cherries; Poppy heads with scarlet paper Poppies; a long stem of Hollyhock with a bright bead of yellow glass glinting inside each seed cup; small artificial bluebirds perched among dried brown stems.

Big and spectacular arrangements can be made with such seed heads as Cow Parsley, Hogweed and their relations; tawny Corn cobs (with 1-foot long leave spread out in enormous star shapes); Globe Artichoke heads, their formal and ornate shape almost demanding to be sprayed gold; and sprays of Beech or other coppery leaves as background material.

If, on the other hand, you like the charm of miniature decorations, look closely at seeds themselves and their markings. In addition to eggcup-size sprays of small seed heads to decorate spots where space is limited, a collection of interesting seeds sorted into envelopes can be used to create patterns on anything from the front of a whitewood chest of drawers to blown eggs (paint first, glue on the seed pattern and varnish). Plain Melon seeds or, indeed, most fruit pips, peppercorns, grains of pearl barley and the contents of a packet of parrot food can all be used for collages.

A selection of some of
the seed heads and leaves
to find and to buy for use
in dried arrangements. Shown
clockwise from left to right
fern (bleached), Cyprus palm,
South African Lily, Wheat,
Lotus, Poppy head, Pine cones,
Thistle head, Wood Lotus and
Protea, with Sweet Corn in the
centre of the picture

gourds

Cucurbita pepo (Gourds), sometimes referred to as Pumpkins in seed catalogues, are usually grown only for decoration. Some are edible but not particularly tasty, while others are definitely unsuitable for human consumption.

Gourds belong to the Cucumber family and are easily grown from seed sown

Dried stems and heads of giant Hogweed (left) in a cylindrical glass vase make an elegant and permanent arrangement. The basket of gourds (below) shows some of the shapes that you can grow. Even in a simple basket the gourds make a charming feature.

in the spring in a box containing John Innes Seed Sowing Compost. When the seedlings are about 2 inches high transfer each one carefully. Plant each one in its own 4-6 inch pot or in a garden in a rich warm soil. The trailing plants need plenty of water and liquid fertilizer, and it is wise to tie the stems up a trellis or strings. Outdoors, support the developing fruits on pieces of wood or slate to prevent slug and moisture damage.

Gourds are usually ripe for picking in the autumn. There are two ways of drying them. Cut them with 4 inch stems attached, tie with string and hang each from a beam or nails in a warm airy place such as an airing cupboard (if not too hot). Alternatively, place the gourds on a wooden tray in a warm room, turning them over from time to time. They will ripen completely in about 14-21 days, becoming much lighter in weight and ready for decora-

tive purposes and arrangements.

To give the fruits a glossy appearance, rub them with linseed oil or varnish. For a high gloss, paint them with clear varnish.

From a packet of mixed ornamental Gourd seeds you will get a number of fruits of various shapes, which can look like marrows, cucumbers, apples, pears, pumpkins and flattened melons. Size will vary considerably and colour will range from pale yellow to dark green, orange and white; often the colours are mixed in curious markings.

Some Gourds have warty skins, which adds to their textural interest. It is also possible to obtain from certain seedsmen packets of seeds of individual species: apple-shaped (pale striped cream), Turban (orange-red, white or yellow flattened 'marrows'), pear-shaped (green and yellow striped), and small pimply hybrids (apple-shaped with multi-coloured; very bumpy skins).

everlasting arrangements

Objets trouvés, things you find lying about, are a great aid to flower arrangements and can make decorative groups on their own or in combination with dried flowers, seed heads, and so on. Many are invaluable additions to groups of indoor plants or miniature gardens.

What you find is likely to depend on the kind of place where you live or go visiting. Holidays and weekend picnics are obvious times to go searching (take a few plastic bags with you specially for the purpose), laying in a store of finds to use in later months. What looks dull underfoot may reveal hidden beauties when at eye level.

Bits of rock, colourful stones, and even chippings used by road menders are worth looking out for. The pinks and reds of granite and snowy quartzite show up well against black slate; and some pieces of stone are made additionally colourful by patches of lichen mottling their surface. Even a chunk of weather-worn brick may be worth bringing home to form the basis of an arrangement. When washed free of dust, the various colours show up better—and a light coat of varnish (from an aerosol spray) may help even more. A group of stones, plus a little Moss and Ivy, could be built round a concealed container with Ferns or other plants, or at the base of an oil lamp which would light them up.

Multicoloured pebbles from a stream can fill a decorative glass jar and support the stems of one or two flowers or a piece of some plant (like Ivy) which will grow happily in water for a long while. The water will make the pebbles glisten.

Sometimes, in ploughed fields or on beaches, you may find huge flints which time has chipped into odd shapes, suggesting some strange animal or bird, or just interesting in an abstract way. With the help of some modelling material (clay or Polyfilla), such a flint can be mounted at a suitable angle on a block of wood, with or without the addition of dried leaves and seed heads around it. Strangely gnarled branches and roots can be treated in a similar way.

Some shingle beaches yield smooth and beautifully rounded pebbles as big as potatoes, with an attraction all their own, either as they are or when sprayed gold, painted with patterns or varnished. Painted patterns are best simple and with only one or two colours. Use poster paint, following the round shape of the pebble and leaving some of the natural stone bare. A group of these, perhaps with 'Straw Daisies' among them, could add a decorative effect in a room where central heating or air conditioning is too intense for fresh flowers or plants. Road mending chips are ordinary but, if examined closely, may be found to have a variety of colours in them—some even sparkle. They serve a useful purpose on top of the compost for indoor plants by conserving moisture. However, you can be creative. Sort them into colours, spray varnish on them and perhaps colour some artificially, using an aerosol spray can of gold paint and one of white (not bright colours that would kill the natural ones). Now use the chips, mosaic-like, to create a simple pattern on, for instance, a 10 inch diameter cakeboard, with a small, shallow, round tin in the centre to hold a few white flower heads. This makes a low but effective centrepiece for a round table. If you want the design to be permanent, first coat the cakeboard with a thin layer of modelling material in which to press the chips or use a rubber adhesive.

Seashells are such an obvious thing to collect that they hardly need mentioning. Cockles can form a border to a miniature garden and a large whelk or scallop shell can have a few tiny plants growing in it, provided all trace of salt water has been washed out first. Using clay or other modelling material as a foundation, dark green candles for the table could have shells and evergreens surrounding their feet. Kitchen foil pressed smoothly over cockles, so that the ribs show through clearly, gives a festive look. A few small silvery glass balls, the kind used for Christmas trees, could be added.

The seashore also yields driftwood, bits of coloured bottle glass worn smooth by the tides, strangely shaped bits of metal, rusty and barnacled, dried bits of seaweed or starfishes, an occasional cork float: a whole treasure-house of *objets trouvés* for the beach-comber.

Mossy logs, gnarled branches, lichen, lengths of bark, weirdly shaped roots, feathers, dry tree fungus, even the bleached skull of a sheep if you have a taste for the slightly macabre—these are the kind of things to look out for in the countryside to add to your hoard of materials which can be used again and again.

Sometimes colours are enhanced by a light spray of varnish, but use this on only selected pieces. To varnish an entire group would ruin the natural look. As a foil to the colours of the more distinctive pieces in a composition a few of those with interesting shapes but flat colours could be sprayed gold (or black, or white—not a colour). As unrelieved gold paint can look boring, a second aerosol of bronze is useful—with a light flick of this, the gold can be given a faintly darker tone here and there.

Natural complements to stone and wood objects are Ferns and other foliage plants or sprigs of evergreens and berries, which will last a long time. Dried or everlasting flowers and seed heads go well with them. Leaves, pressed for a week between the pages of a book, are another good complement—particularly in the rich colours of autumn.

About modelling materials

These are useful as a base into which to push sticks, stones and stems to hold them in place. Plasticine is clean, re-usable and available in unobtrusive colours. Clay dries hard and can then be painted if wished; use it in solid lumps or it will crumble as it dries. Polyfilla plaster (sold for filling cracks in walls) can be mixed to a dough-like consistency with just a little water and it dries hard. Toy shops sell various modelling doughs for children. A homely version can be made with flour and water plus salt to strengthen it and it is strong enough for most purposes: it dries hard and can be painted.

An everlasting arrangement for a wall-panel. This splendid trophy is made mainly out of objects collected in Australia, and the whole design was carefully planned before any work was started. Remember that if you wish to hang the panel, you should put a screw or hook in the board before you begin

Materials for a wall-panel
— board, tape, Polyfilla, grasses etc.

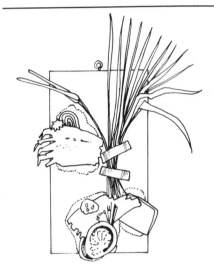

Use sticky tape to fix stems
and Polyfilla for solid objects

Continue adding materials until the
board is hidden and the panel complete

how plants improve a home

When you are incorporating pot plants into the decorative scheme of a room, the same considerations of taste apply as in flower arranging. Is the style of the room formal or informal, rustic or sophisticated, cosy or austere? The choice and arrangement of plants should follow suit.

There are, of course, other considerations to keep in mind. Plants are more permanent than cut flowers and some grow to be big, so scale is very important. There is less choice about their placement because many need light, a steady temperature and minimal handling.

Some demand a prominent position when in flower, but if their foliage is uninteresting they may need to be moved into obscurity until the next blooming season. Concealed pots of water containing cut flowers can be used to replace the splash of colour.

As with flowers, one massed array is often more effective than pots here and there, provided there is space. But leaves are a permanent feature, so it is important to group together interestingly contrasted foliage—slender and round, fleshy and lacy, upright and trailing, glossy and velvety. Shape may be a more important consideration than colour.

Unless some plants in a group are naturally taller than others, pots at the back can be raised up (empty food cans, well concealed, are useful for this purpose).

If the arrangement is below eye-level, the view from above will be most important, but if it will be seen most often from low armchairs, check how it looks from this angle too. Remember that small plants with delicate blooms will be wasted unless they are near eye-level.

A mass of one kind of flowering plant can provide a dramatic colour accent in a room. A variety of plants and colours will be most successful against a very plain background. In a room with patterned wallpaper or fabrics, it may be best to stick to white flowers or foliage plants—and essential if the group is not near the window.

The massing of plants can be accomplished by putting several pots together inside a larger container (like an old preserving pan or Victorian washbasin) or in a trough, or by grouping them.

A shelf above a radiator would be suitable for a group of plants that like dry warmth; a cool, empty grate for Ferns; a tiered table or dumbwaiter for a mixture of upright and trailing plants; even a tea trolley or saucepan rack can be adapted. A jardinière (of bamboo or decorative white ironwork, for instance) is a purpose-made solution to the problem.

A whole bay window might be filled with plants, particularly if the view beyond is dull. A mantlepiece could be topped with a made-to-measure tray, provided the plants will not be over-heated by a fire below. It may be worth fitting wooden steps into a corner or an alcove, so that pot plants can descend, terrace-style, down to floor level.

If a room is too small or crowded for a massed group, there may be a corner where one tall plant can stand on its own; or a striking climber can be encouraged to travel along the top of a bookcase or a beam or decorate a picture rail. A number of such plants are happy in corners with relatively little light. These deserve handsome urns, tubs or containers that can be part of the furniture of the room.

Alternatively, choose a plant that will stay small, put it in a really interesting container, and give it pride of place on a desk or table where its detail can be seen. If a small plant is to occupy an important spot, it needs particularly attractive leaves or flowers or growing habits that are interesting to watch—like *Saxifraga sarmentosa* (Mother of Thousands) and its babies or *Tolmiea menziessii* (Pig-a-back Plant), which produces little leaves on top of the old ones. Two small plants, each in a square container, could serve as bookends. Another solution, when space is short, is to hang a group of wall pots containing plants that trail or to fill the shelves of a tall bookcase with plants or to use a long trough in front of a blocked-in fireplace.

Some rooms are necessarily bare of furniture—narrow entrance halls, for instance, and bathrooms. Suitable plants can 'clothe' these places, and make them seem less empty. If the lines of such a room are straight, the natural curving shape of most plants can lessen the stark effect.

On a dinner table, use low plants in conjunction with candles instead of cut flowers. For example, pink African Violets with tall candles to match the flowers make a charming combination (but use kitchen foil at the bottom to ensure that the candles will not burn low and harm the plants). Or the plants might be grouped around a small white china figurine.

Miniature dish gardens are suitable for coffee tables, where their detail can be enjoyed at close quarters, particularly if there is a lamp nearby to light them at night. Such an arrangement will be seen from all sides, so it needs to be attractive all round, with the tallest plants in the middle.

Grouping plants

When choosing flowering plants to put together, try to get a good contrast of shapes without a great mixture of colours. Shade and sun-loving plants are not good partners nor should one include fast growers which will soon swamp their neighbours. Decide whether you want them to flower simultaneously or in succession. For a fairly small bowl, a threesome may be the most to aim for—one tall, one spreading, and one trailing low in the foreground. Large tubs or urns demand plants with some stature. In troughs, try alternating short and tall plants, with most of the height in the centre; a small trellis standing against a wall could be added for a climber at the back of the trough. Here are some possible groupings:

For a painted tub or urn in a cool light hall: a white Marguerite with trailing white ivy-leaved *Pelargonium peltatum* (Geraniums) at its feet makes a striking summer display.

For a trough in a warm, dry room: *Bromeliads, Clivia, Hibiscus* and *Hoya Carnosa*, a climber—the pinks and reds make a dramatic summer show.

Shade-loving plants for a wide bowl in a warm room: red *Anthurium* with white African Violets at its feet and a red *Columnea* trailing over the edge. These all have flowers which should be at eye-level for their detail to be appreciated.

Massed foliage plants arranged in a traditional style create a charming, if rather Victorian atmosphere, and lead the eye naturally into the garden.

A spring group for a cool, shady spot: line a bread basket with plastic and plant yellow *Calceolarias*, yellow and blue *Primulas* and some Ivy.

For a bookcase, a tray of pebbles and water with a row of pots containing trailing flowers, such as *Campanula isophylla*, *Tradescantia* and *Columnea*. For a permanent room divider, a decorative screen of bamboo trellis set in a trough filled with plants. Suitable climbers such as *Passiflora* (Passion Flower), Jasmine and *Bougainvillea* can be intermingled with foliage creepers such as *Cissus antarctica*, *Testrastigma*,

Monstera deliciosa and *Rhoicissus rhomboidea* (Grape Ivy), all of which are evergreen. Below could go a permanent covering of plants such as *Tradescantia*, *Saxifraga sarmentosa*, *Helxine soleirollii* and *Fittonia*, with flowering plants in pots added from time to time.

Green plants, Marguerites and Hydrangeas (above) add interest to an unused hearth. The illustration (right) shows how a large room can be transformed by using a massive plant constructively, but remember that growing and manipulating a plant on this scale will take time

The easy plants

Some plants, luckily, are happy in almost any conditions. If every pot plant you were given in the past died almost as soon as you looked at it, do not lose heart. Try some of the plants listed below—they are virtually impossible to kill.

The *Aspidistra Elatior* used to be called the cast-iron plant as it happily survived in gas-lit interiors with coal fires. It has dark green leaves, and is happy anywhere except in full sun.

Beloperone Guttata (Shrimp Plant) is a small shrub which comes from South America. It has light green leaves and coppery shrimp-shaped bracts covering its tiny, insignificant white flowers. Prune it in the spring to encourage a bushy shape and, if possible, place it in a very well-lit position.

Chlorophytum Comosum (the Spider Plant) has long green and white grass-like leaves falling like a fountain, and baby plants appearing on the end of runners. These can be easily rooted around the parent plant. Or root them in separate pots, then cut them off and you have another house plant.

The varieties of *Cissus*—*Cissus Antarctica* (Kangaroo Vine) and *Rhoicissus Rhomboidea* (Grape Ivy)—are easy climbing or trailing plants. They are happiest in shady, tolerably cool, conditions.

Coleus (Ornamental Nettle) have no relationship to the Stinging Nettle except the ragged shape of their leaves. This large family of plants all have ornamental variegated leaves in reds, yellows, purples and greens. They need good light—otherwise their leaf markings fade—and frequent watering. It is a good idea to pinch out the growing point and remove the flower buds to encourage a bushy shape. Their flowers are not really attractive and take too much nourishment from the plant itself —it is the leaves which are important.

The three members of the *Ficus* or Fig family easiest to grow are *Ficus Benjamina* (Weeping Fig) which is a delicate little tree with greyish bark and long narrow leaves; *Ficus Elastica* (Rubber Plant) which has a tall, classic appearance due to the broad, leathery leaves, and *Ficus Pumila* (Creeping Fig) whose small round leaves creep and trail. This plant has to be supported by tying it to a cane if you do not want it to hang down.

Hederas (Ivies) are a large family of climbing or trailing plants with decorative leaves. Ivies are as hardy in the house as in the garden, being happy in cool or warm rooms. But remember the warmer the room, the more light and humidity they need.

Tradescantia (Wandering Sailor) do not seem to mind what soil, temperature or position they grow in—although some of the silver and green striped varieties show their colours better in semi-shade. They will trail down from a high shelf or wall in a curtain of pointed striped leaves and are very easy to propagate from cuttings. *Zebrinas* (members of the same family and also known as Wandering Sailor) are similar in appearance and are happy in the same conditions. The underside of the leaf is a beautiful deep purple, particularly if the plant is kept fairly dry.

Plants for a cool room

Ideal for a cool, light room are plants which do not mind a lack of warm sunlight as long as they receive sufficient day-light.

Aechmea Rhodocyanea (Urn Plant or Exotic Bush) has silvery grey-green curving leaves and produces an amazing pink bracted flower which lasts for months.

Some varieties of *Chrysanthemum* are now available in pots to grow indoors. These make good house plants as they are reasonably hardy and flower throughout the year.

Impatiens (Busy Lizzie) is a popular plant with iridescent orange, red or pink flowers and green or crimson tinged leaves depending upon the variety. It flowers more if it is put in a very light place. Pinch out the growing shoots occasionally to keep the plant bushy. In summer give it a lot of water, in winter only a little. Cuttings taken in the summer root easily in water.

Sansevieria Trifasciata (Mother-in-Law's Tongue) has erect, strong, leathery leaves. It needs very little water, does not like being damp in winter (its roots rot very easily if it is) and prefers a well-lit situation.

Sparmannia Africana (Zimmer-Linden, House Lime or African Hemp) has large, soft, pale green, furry leaves and produces pretty white flowers in early spring. It can grow up to 6 feet or more but, by picking out the growing point, can be made to bush out. This plant needs to be well watered and should be in a light airy position. In winter it prefers a cool place, and in summer, if it is not too big to move, will benefit from being transferred to a shady place outside.

Plants for a warm room

If your room is warm choose some of the plants listed below. But if you have central heating make sure there is enough humidity for them, they all need moisture.

Asparagus is not really a fern. It is, in fact, as you can see by its fine feathery leaves closely related to vegetable asparagus. It needs moisture, and a reasonably warm situation, and benefits from a spell in good light during the summer.

The *Bromeliads* (Air Pines) are a large family, of which the pineapple is one, whose striped and coloured leaves grow in a stiff rosette or crown forming a cup in the centre. Put water in this central cup, and keep the soil damp. They are epiphytes (living on trees and roofs) so can be grown in small pots and do not need repotting. They are happy in sun or shade, although the more light they receive the better the shadings of their leaves, and they do not mind too much if they are neglected for days on end. The three types of *Bromeliad* mentioned below ideally should be put somewhere low so that their stiff sculptural shapes can be seen from above.

Bilbergia Nutans has long, narrow, dark-green leaves and an unbelievable flower cluster of green, blue and red.

Cryptanthus are dwarf bromeliads without the central cup; they are flat like tabby starfish, striped silver and purple, tolerant and easy-going if kept in a moist atmosphere.

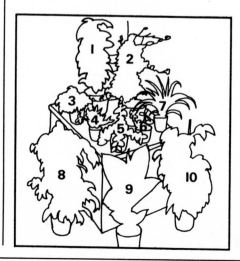

Neoregelia Carolinae Tricolor forms a large flat rosette, has long narrow sword-shaped leaves striped cream and pink and is happy in shade.

There are many varieties of *Dieffenbachia* (Dumb Cane), some of which have ornamental leaves with yellow or cream patterning and green edges. All must be sheltered from draughts.

Ferns vary as to the amount of warmth they need, but they all need very little light and a moist atmosphere. This, unfortunately, makes a lot of them unsuitable as house plants. But here are two which are reasonably easy to grow in a warm room as long as they do not get too much light.

Adiantum (Maidenhair Fern) is somewhat delicate but so attractive and ornamental that it is well-worth taking trouble with. Keep it away from draughts—which it particularly dislikes—and make sure it is not in a dry atmosphere. Either spray it once or more a day or stand the pot on an inverted saucer in a bowl of water. Keep the soil as well as the atmosphere moist.

Asplenium Nidus (Bird's Nest Fern) has bright green leaves with dark mid-ribs. It is happier in a rather warm temperature and, again, must be kept moist.

Sinningia (Gloxinia) with its large dark leaves and velvety bell-shaped flowers is one of the most attractive house plants and flowers throughout the summer.

Schefflera Actinophylla (Umbrella Tree, Sunray Plant) is a shrubby plant with glossy green leaves which divide into between three to seven 'fingers'. It grows quite tall—between three and four feet—and does not mind a semi-shaded position, but must be kept moist. (It will shed its leaves if it is allowed to dry out.)

A collection of pot plants which will survive in most conditions:
1 *Cissus Antartica (Kangaroo Vine)*
2 *Hedera Helix (Variegated Ivy)*
3 *Beloperone Guttata (Shrimp Plant)*
4 *Silver Tradescantia (Wandering Sailor)*
5 *Ficus Pumila (Creeping Fig)*
6 *Zebrina Purpurea (Wandering Sailor)*
7 *Chlorophytum Comosum Variegatum (Spider Plant)*
8 *Ficus Benjamina (Weeping Fig)*
9 *Ficus Robusta (Rubber Plant)*
10 *Rhoicissus Rhomboidea (Grape Ivy)*
And a collection of Coleus (Ornamental Nettle) (right) with the leaves of the Aspidistra Eliator (far right).

Plants suitable for a cool room (below and top right):
1. *Aechmea Rhodocyanea* (Urn Plant, Exotic Brush)
2. *Sansevieria Trifasciata Laurentii* (Mother-in-Law's Tongue)
3. *Impatiens Petersiana* (Dusky Lizzie)
4. *Ayr Xant* (Chrysanthemum)

Below the Sparmannia Africana (Zimmer-Linden, House Lime, African Hemp)

Plants suitable for a warm room (below and centre left):
1. Schefflera Actinophylla (Umbrella Tree, Sunray Plant)
2. Asparagus Fern
3. Adianthum (Maidenhair Fern)
4. Cryptanthus/Dracana Bromeliad (Air Pine)
5. Sinningia (Gloxinia)
6. Asplenium Nidus (Bird's Nest Fern)
7. Dieffenbachia (Dumb Cane)

growing cacti and succulents

The weird shapes of these fleshy plants are an endless source of fascination, especially when exotic flowers bloom on them. The flowers of cacti are particularly exquisite and brilliant. Some grow like single stars, some in clusters or circlets. But do not be surprised if some only flower every seven years or so: they are worth waiting for!

They thrive on neglect and are almost the only plants that need no watering when you go on holdiay. In addition, they are untroubled by central heating or air conditioning.

Cacti come from desert places where rainfall is infrequent, and the plants are designed to absorb rapidly any moisture that comes their way and to store it. The last thing they need is soggy soil or a damp atmosphere. A number of other succulents (fleshy-leaved plants) share these characteristics, but not all.

Care

Those bought in pots will already be in the kind of compost they like. If you transplant, mix into some John Innes Potting Compost No. 2 an equal volume of sand, or buy a bag of special cactus compost. Once a year remove the top inch of old compost and put new in — or, if the cactus has grown much, put it in a larger pot of new compost. This is better than giving fertilizer.

Cacti (and some other succulents which need the same conditions) like to have more water when growing than when resting. Most grow in the summer (the Zygocactus, which flowers at Christmas, is an exception), and need very little attention in winter except to keep the soil from drying out completely. Only *Lithops* prefer dry soil in winter. Do not water on really cold days. If the surface of the compost is caked, break it up gently to let the water through. Occasionally, stand the pot in water for half an hour then drain very throughly. As spring progresses increase the water gradually. How often you water will depend on the weather: in a cool summer, once a week would do, in a hot one water might be needed daily. Either too much or too little water can cause brown patches or softness of the plants. Occasionally, turn the pots round so that the plants grow evenly.

The more sunshine the better — particularly in the fresh air during summer rather than behind glass (though a south-facing window-sill is ideal in summer). But in cold, damp weather, cacti are at their most vulnerable and should be put in a fairly warm, light and airy place away from draughts: few window sills are safe in winter.

Repot when the plant gets too big (the method is the same for any other plant) but always do this in warm weather. Another job for a warm day is syringing any plants that are dusty.

Display

Small cacti are very suitable for miniature gardens. A porous container or one with drainage holes is essential. Don't mix cacti with other succulents unless their growing needs are the same: some have different light, water and compost needs.

Another way to arrange a collection of suitable cacti is to use a window-like display case, provided it is sunny and draughtproof. A shelf could be built out from the sill, or a series of small shelves put in at each side, equipped with plastic drip trays of the same size. The trays should be filled with gravel or pebbles so that the pots do not stand in their own drips after watering. Or build a glazed framework outside a sash window and use this as a small conservatory. In winter leave one sash open at night so that the warmth of the room reaches the plants. It is also important to cover the outside glass at night (with paper or other material) to prevent the external cold affecting the plants. Some cacti and succulents suitable for growing indoors are:

Haworthias. Dark green to brown stemless rosettes of leaves, some varieties looking rather like Pine cones. Flowers are greenish-white, small and appear to have lips. These succulents prefer shade, otherwise they are easy to grow.

Aloes. Very mixed group of plants, varying from dwarf rosettes of leaves to almost tree-like specimens and climbers. Flowers are usually tubular, orange or red and borne on long central stems. Very tolerant plants to grow under the general conditions described above.

Gasterias. Extremely popular because they are easy to grow. Stemless leaves, dark green to brown with attractive white markings, often grow sideways from each other, not forming a complete rosette. Reddish, green-tipped flowers are carried on long curving stems.

Rebutias. A beginner's delight, they grow easily and flower freely. They are bright green, dwarf, clustered plants. Sometimes webby and sometimes spiny, they have stemless flowers in various shades of red and yellow.

Opuntias. Varied genus in appearance, the most common varieties usually having large, flat, green, spiny or hairy stems which grow out of each other to give a sculptured appearance. The open flowers — red or yellow — grow straight from these and are produced freely. Some even fruit and a few are edible.

Epiphyllums (previously called *Phyllocactus*). Leaf-like green stems, sometimes with prickles, and large flowers open during the day. The flowers are usually red though some hybrids are white. Each has several petals, and more flowers buds follow on the short flower stem. They are easy to grow, but require regular watering when in flower, usually spring/early summer.

Zygocactus. Commonly called Christmas Cactus, as it produces large tubular red flowers freely during the winter. Stems are green and leaf-like, frequently curving over the edge of the pot. It needs water and liquid fertiliser regularly when the flower buds form. Very easy to grow.

Notocactus. Green-brown 'columns', usually heavily covered with spines, which freely produce many-petalled flowers. One of the easiest Cacti to grow and very popular.

Mammillaria. Large and easy to grow, with plants usually forming single circular clumps, occasionally producing small off shoots. One or two varieties are more columnear in shape but all produce rings of red, yellow or white flowers regularly each year.

Lithops. Commonly called Stone or Pebble Plants, their greeny brown and white marked shapes are similiar in size and contour. Usually they grow in clumps of white or yellow flowers. It is important to keep them dry during their 'resting time' from winter to early summer.

Echinocactus, Very spiny, tall, ribbed, circular plants, they produce flowers rarely when artificially cultivated, but are otherwise easy to grow. Best known is *E. grusonii*, with its golden yellow spines. A little lime added to the compost is beneficial.

Chamaecereus. Attractive low growing plants with rounded prickly branched stems producing scarlet/orange tubular flowers each year. They should be handled with care as the stems are brittle, but they root from broken pieces.

Kalenchoe. Easy to grow but they like richer and more moist compost than most cacti and succulents. They vary in height, but can grow up to 6 feet and produce attractive leaves of green, grey or brown on short or long stems, according to variety. Flowers are usually red and borne in clusters.

Echeveria. Rosettes of multi-coloured leaves with a variety of shapes are produced at soil level or on stems several inches tall. The plants in this easy-growing group are as attractive out of flower as in bloom. The blossoms are usually a reddish colour.

Euphorbia. The vast family of *Euphorbiacea* produces many types of plants as well as a few succulents. The latter are so varied in form as to be almost impossible to describe in general. They may be tree-like, have leaf stems, be columnear, look like leaves, be very spiny, have some normal simple leaves, or produce single or clusters of flowers in various colours. Normal cacti and succulent growing conditions will suit them all.

The different cacti shown below are (clockwise from left to right): Haworthia attenuata (Lily of the Veld), Euphorbia submammillaris (Devil's Pin Cushion), Aloe ferox (Big Bopper), Opuntia sublata (Tequilla Tango), Rebutia senilis (Tijuana Tornado) and, in the centre, Opuntia microdasys (Bunny Ears)

ferns

Ferns have a strange charm of their own. Used in groups, they can be very decorative, the lacy fronds of some contrasting with the long tongue-like leaves of others. The Victorians, who did not have the problems of central heating or air conditioning to worry about, were fond of indoor ferneries or rocky grottoes planted with Ferns, an idea worth reviving if a cool enough spot can be found in the more comfortable homes of today. An empty grate might be ideal. Alternatively, there are Ferns from tropical forests which like a steamy atmosphere.

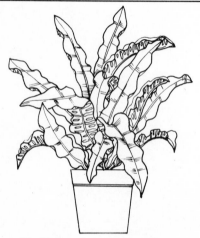

Phyllitis scolopendrium crispum
(Hart's Tongue Fern)

Coming from dim forest glades, Ferns do not need much light, which is a considerable help in some corners of the house. But they do need moist conditions—either lots of watering or the humid atmosphere of an enclosed glass case or bottle garden.

You can collect Ferns from a wood, or possibly growing at the foot of a town wall, but pot-grown plants from a plant nursery are likely to do better indoors.

Although they need plenty of moisture, the usual drainage precautions must be taken to keep their roots from getting soggy.

To keep Ferns healthy grow them, if possible, in a mixture consisting of equal parts of sand, peat and compost; a handful of leaf mould would be a helpful addition.

It is not always easy to buy Ferns as pot plants and choice may be limited, but some are worth looking out for.

Asplenium (Spleenworts). A large genus of evergreen Ferns which vary considerably in appearance. Leaves are leathery in texture and the plants strong growing, which helps them withstand a variety of conditions. However, very small *Aspleniums* need special care and thrive in Ward cases. Most cultivated varieties are decorative with typical fern-like fronds. *A.bulbiflorum* has lovely green fronds 2 feet long and 8 inches wide; *A.colensoi* has young plants on its 9 inch fronds; and *A.trichomanes* (Maidenhair Spleenwort), with its tufted 6-12 inch fronds, is hardy and will withstand tough conditions.

Asplenium nidus is one of the exceptions in the group as it has single undivided leaves (not frond-like) which can grow as long as 4 feet and be 6-9 inches across. It does, however need warm, moist conditions to flourish.

Adiantum (Maidenhair Fern). Another genus containing many handsome forms. In general, the 'leaflets' are more rounded than the *Aspleniums* and the plants more graceful and delicate. Most species are hardy and easy to grow and keep well indoors. *A.cuneatum* and *A.capillus-veneris* require little attention; the latter is particularly attractive with almost clover-like 'leaflets'. Both varieties grow about 9 inches long.

Nephrolepis (Ladder Ferns). Delightful ferns, all with simple 'leaflet' fronds which can grow up to 4 feet long. Allow them plenty of space to develop. They are particularly effective when grouped among other ferns and are very useful in hanging baskets, as all tend to droop. The most popular are *N.acuminata* and *N.exaltata*.

Phyllitis. Among the few Ferns in this genus *P.scolopendrium* (Hart's Tongue), and its varieties, is by far the most

Asparagus
(Asparagus Fern)

popular. The fronds are single and strap-shaped, growing up to 18 inches in length. Their beautiful green contrasts effectively with other Ferns in a group. It is variable in form, however, and it is worth looking for the particular shape and appearance you like.

Pteris. A large genus, all with graceful fronds of many 'leaflets'. The best varieties for indoor growing, especially as they tolerate light better than many other ferns, are *P.cretica* (fronds 6-12 inches); *P.multifida*, the Spider Fern (up to 18 inches); and *P.tremula*

Adiantum
(Maidenhair Fern)

(fronds of up to 4 feet long and 2 feet wide, so allow it plenty of space to grow to its full glory).

Platycerium (Stag's or Elk's Horn Fern). Perhaps the most extraordinary of all Ferns. Their common names describes the appearance. Known as ephiphytic Ferns, they grow well in baskets or fastened to a piece of wood or tree branch with wire or string. In both cases wrap their roots in coarse peat and sphagnum moss. They like plenty of light, and water in moderation. The most commonly found variety is *P.bifurcatum*.

Asparagus (Asparagus Fern). It is not a true fern but is mentioned here because of its delicate green feathery foliage and climbing habit (up to 10 feet). *A.plumosus* and *A.sprengeri* are the two most popular. They like plenty of water and liquid fertilizer in summer and will stand light better than many true ferns. Excellent for baskets and cutting for flower arrangements.

The lightness and delicacy of many ferns make them particularly attractive as house plants. In the photograph (right) the outlines of the fronds are thrown into relief by the white background

large plants

Outsize plants are well suited to a large room, but can also turn any blank corner into an important feature. One on its own may be all that is needed to give an entrance hall character or to divert the eye away from a dull view through a window behind it. A big climber could conceal a multitude of architectural sins or help to enhance a good feature such as a well-proportioned archway or door frame.

Climbers can also be trained up tall moss covered posts, kept damp to give their leaves the moisture they appreciate. Keep the damp posts away from walls or furniture.

There are a number of large plants that can be used individually for room decoration. Most of them are evergreen with the foliage in various colours, but they rarely flower. Among the more common ones are *Monstera*, *Philodendron* (climbing and non-climbing varieties), *Cissus*, *Schefflera* and *Rhoicissus*. There are others equally easy to grow which can make delightful permanent features in a room. These could include:

Howea (Synonym Kentia) *H. belmoreana* (6-10 feet) and *H. fosteriana* (8-15 feet) are the two most commonly grown, for their graceful feathery shaped

Rhoicissus rhomboidea

leaves are rather like those of the Date Palm. They need large containers, good compost and a room temperature of about 60°F. These 'palms' prefer light but not direct sun, plenty of water spring to autumn and liquid fertiliser but less moisture in winter. Sponge the leaves weekly to keep them clean and healthy.

Dasylirion. Palm-like evergreens related to Yuccas. They have short stems and long, tough, leather leaves with spiny margins. As the plants grow (upright for about 1½ feet), the older lower leaves bend downwards, the new ones continue upwards, and the plant develops a 'waisted' appearance. Growing conditions are similiar to those required for *Howea*, but temperatures can be lower.

Phoenix (Date Palm). Most varieties

Phoenix roebelinii
(*Palm*)

are too large for the home but *P.acaulis* (8-12 feet) and *P.roebelinii* (4-6 feet) with their drooping, dark green fronds of leathery leaves are very decorative. Grow similarly to the previous two 'Palms', except to ensure that the temperature never falls below 65°F (18°C).

Ficus (Rubber Plants and Figs). There are many large growing forms — tree-like and climbing — suitable for indoor growing. *F.elastica* (the India Rubber Plant) is probably best known for its tree shape (up to 12 feet) and dark green, glossy, large leaves. Its varieties *F.decora* and *F.doescheri* are even more attractive. The leaves of the former have red undersurfaces and leaf sheaths, while the latter has pale green leaves with cream markings, white margins and pale pink leaf sheaths. *Ficus*

Ficus elastica
(*India Rubber Tree*)

lyrate, (Fiddle Back Fig) is another decorative form, growing in a 'chunky' fashion with large violin shaped leaves. *F.pumila*, (Climbing Fig) has smaller leaves and will grow rapidly up supports as a screen. All Figs like semi-shade, a good general compost, plenty of water in summer but little in winter, and withstand coolish conditions but not draughts. Sponge leaves occasionally in summer.

Tetrastigma, (Chinese or Chestnut Vine). A fast growing climber with vigorous tendrils and large, green compound leaves like Horse Chestnut. It needs a large room, where it can be trained up supports to make an overhead feature or a living room divider. It likes light but not bright sun, its compost evenly moist all year round, and liquid fertiliser in summer.

Datura. Not often seen as houseplants but they can be grown indoors in large containers, especially two of the shrubby perennial varieties — *D.arborea* and *D.suaveolens* (both with the common name of Angel's Trumpet). They have large clusters of leaves near the top of the stems and in summer produce 8-12 inch long tubular white drooping flowers. They look similar, though the latter variety is larger. Normal compost, water and fertiliser in summer, little water in winter, pruning to shape in early autumn, moderate light and a period outdoors in the summer if possible, are the main requirements.

An elegant drawing-room decorated with soft, warm tones has a tall graceful Howea and an orange tree for a touch of colour

flowering plants for spring

With a little planning, it is possible to have plants flowering in the home throughout the year. These pages show a choice for every season.

Due to modern plant growing techniques, it is often possible to buy pot plants in bloom outside their normal season (Chrysanthemums, African Violets, and some Azaleas, for instance). But the ordinary home gardener cannot achieve these results and must observe the natural seasons of the plants.

There are a large number of flowering plants to add colour to the home but, unfortunately, many have a short life under artificial growing conditions. *Anthuriums, Chrysanthemums, Azaleas, Impatiens* (Busy Lizzie), *Pelargoniums* and *Aphelandra*, for example, can be kept for two years or more, if they get the attention they like. But others should be nurtured only for their colour and temporary beauty, to add to a collection of foliage plants or to brighten things up when you feel something new and living could make a difference. As a guide to some of the many plants available, the following have been divided into their flowering seasons of spring, summer and autumn/winter. Other seasonal flowering plants will be found in other sections of this book.

Spring Flowering Plants

Anthurium (Flamingo Plant). Evergreen tropical plant, about 3 feet high, which requires a warm, moist, shady atmosphere and a minimum temperature of 60°F (15.5°C) to grow well. It is dramatic, with its large, glossy variegated or green leaves and colourful leaf-like flower with a pimply tail sticking out of the middle. There are various forms — *A. andreanum* (scarlet and white), *A. scherzerianum* (scarlet), *A. ornatum* (white and purple) and others produced by specialist growers. Anthuriums can be kept for foliage effects alone.

Primula. There are a great number of these which can be obtained during most of the year, but the late winter and early spring varieties remain in bloom for several weeks and are the most popular. Common species include *P. obconica,* with large primrose-like flowers and hairy leaves which can

cause a skin rash on some people; *P. malacoides*, with smaller blooms; *P. kewensis*, with tubular flowers, and *P. sinensis* with largish blooms.

Primulas produce their clusters of blooms in various shades of yellow, blue, red, pink or white on longish stems above the primrose-like leaves. Water and feed freely when in flower and remove dead heads; keep in a light, draught-free position in a temperature of 55°-60°F (about 15°C). Primulas are bushy plants, up to 2 feet high.

Hydrangea. The common forms are usually species of *H. macrophylla hortensis*, which produce large globular flower heads in shades of pink, red or blue in spring and early summer. Pot-grown plants usually reach about 2-3 feet, but if planted in tubs and given the summer outdoors, heights of up to 8 feet can be reached. Staking is generally necessary, but these can be hidden by the large veined leaves. Keep Hydrangeas in a light, airy place in a cool room, water and feed during the flowering period — with rain water if possible as Hydrangeas dislike lime. Prune old stems after flowering to encourage young growth to ripen for next year.

Begonia. Of the many types of Begonias those most usually grown for spring and early summer flowers are the fibrous-rooted varieties. Single flowers in shades of red, pink and white are produced in small clusters and look particularly effective against the shiny, small, dark green leaves. Remove dead heads, water well when in flower and keep at 55°F (13°C). in a light room.

These plants stay healthier if their pots are put in an outer container of moist peat. Useful spring flower varieties are *B. acutifolia* (white), *B. foliosa* (white and rose), *B. hydrocotylifolia* (pink) and most

commonly *B. semperflorens* (large pink flowers with reddish leaves).

Impatiens (Busy Lizzie). This plant produces red, pink or white flowers from spring through autumn and is rarely without some colour in its blooms or leaves throughout the year. It has fleshy, brittle stems and smallish leaves and can grow to a large bushy size. However, it is most effective if the stems are pinched back to keep the plant compact and full of flowers. Easy to grow under most conditions, Busy Lizzie does like plenty of sun. It can easily be rooted from stem cuttings in water.

Calceolaria (Slipper Flower). Clusters of 'pouched' flowers, usually yellow, white, red or orange with brown or purple spots, are carried just above the veined and slightly furry leaves in spring and early summer. The plants grow 9-12 inches tall, require plenty of water and a light airy position. Discard after flowering, and select plant for colour and form when buying.

Rosa. Large Roses are not suitable for pot-growing in the home, but the miniature varieties are a charming feature in spring and summer, grown singly or grouped together. They grow only 6-12 inches tall and produce single or double flowers profusely if well-watered in a warm sunny position. Dead heads should be removed to encourage fresh blooms. There are many varieties to choose from in a range of white, pink, yellow, orange, red and lilac. After flowering, either discard or plant outdoors in the garden for the future.

Chrysanthemum frutescens (Paris Daisy or Marguerite). An unusual plant which grows to be a 2½-foot-high shrub. It produces attractive white or yellow daisy-like flowers almost continually from later winter until late summer. Water moderately, but feed well while in flower and keep the temperature about 55°F (13°C). In autumn cut out the older stems which have flowered to allow new growth. When the plant becomes straggly and has few flowers, discard it or try to raise new ones from basal stem cuttings.

Illustrated right: Hydrangea (above), Anthurium andreanum (below left), Primula obonica (below right)

flowering plants for summer

Pelargonium There is often confusion about which plants are Geraniums and which are *Pelargoniums*. The basic differences are that most Geraniums are garden perennials (not pot-plants) and they produce a seed pod which looks like a crane's bill (hence their common name). *Pelargoniums* are pot-plants which differ in form, leaf and flower. Generally the latter grow 2-3 feet high but some can be trained quite well up a trellis. The leaves may be green and oval-shaped or ivy-like with serrated edges, but frequently they are more rounded and plain green or variegated with yellow, white, brown or orange margins or circles. The flowers are borne in trusses and may simply consist of five petals opening out horizontally or in a double layer, while others are almost trumpet-shaped or consist of a mass of petals with serrated edges or quill shapes. Basically *Pelargoniums* are divided into three groups: the Species, which have small flowers and green scented leaves: the Regals with larger flowers and mainly green leaves; and the Zonals which have variagated leaves and the largest range of flower forms. *Pelargoniums* flower freely throughout the summer in shades of white, pink, orange, red, purple or mixed colours. They like plenty of sun, water and fertiliser when in flower, a moderate temperature, and almost dry conditions in winter. Dead flower heads should be removed. To encourage flowering the following year, cut back the stems in winter. These are ideal plants for pots, tubs, and hanging baskets (some varieties trail), but the selection of plant type is a matter of personal choice, with such a large range of varieties and species from which to choose.

Beloperone. The most commonly grown is *B.guttata*, the Shrimp Plant, which grows 2-3 feet high and produces reddish, leaf-like bracts which enclose the white flowers and remain for a long period, looking like decorative shrimps. This bushy plant with arching flower stems likes plenty of light (out of direct sunlight), water in summer and warm conditions in winter.

Aphelandra. Evergreen plant, 2-3 feet tall, which requires warmth, light but not draughts, ample water and a moist atmosphere in summer, and feeding when the flower buds form in late spring. The best known is *A. squarrosa louisae*, which produces yellow spikes of blooms and has large leaves marked strikingly along the midrib and veins an ivory-white colour. The red flowered varieties are rarely seen and more difficult to grow. Always remove dead flowers and cut the stems back to 2 inches at the end of winter to encourage new growth.

Fuchsia. Sometimes called Lady's Eardrops because of their complex, colourful hanging flowers borne from late spring through the summer months. The flowers are sometimes of one colour

Spathiphyllum wallisii
(*White Sails*)

but usually of two or more—generally in shades of white, pink, yellow, red, purple and violet and often brilliant in their intensity. The pot plants can be purchased in various forms — small bush trained, trailing (cascade varieties), standards (a single stem grows 3 feet high before the side shoots are allowed to form a bushy head), and fan-trained up strings or canes. The foliage is usually a lovely green with the veins and leaf stems coloured red. There are a mass of varieties and species to choose from, and selection is essentially a personal matter. *Fuchias* are easy to grow, requiring warmth, light, and plenty of food and water when in flower and a cool airy room and virtually dry soil in the winter. Remove dead heads and keep the plant to the required shape by pruning and pinching out shoots in spring.

Celosia (Cockscomb). The common name is derived from the feathery plumes of vibrant yellow, red, orange or pink flowers which rise above the leaves of green or russet-brown. These annuals (throw away after flowering) grow 1-3 feet high and are very decorative room plants. Strains usually grown are *C. argentea*, *C. plumosa*, *C. cristata*.

Campanula. This genus consists mainly of outdoor plants but the charming *C. pyramidalis* (Bellflower) growing 4-5 feet with lovely tubular white or lavender flowers, and *C. isophylla* and its varieties, with its trailing cascades of open white or pale blue blooms, are two delightful plants for the home, especially if the latter is in a hanging basket. Cool conditions, good light, regular summer watering, removal of dead flower heads and cutting back after blooming should keep this plant happy and floriferous.

Spathiphyllum. An unusual plant resembling an *Anthurium* or Arum Lily. Its green, leaf-like flower has a green-white seedy 'tail' projection rising from among glossy green leaves. *S. wallisii* (6-12 inches) is the variety grown most often but it is not an easy plant and needs shade, frequent feeding, regular re-potting and a minimum temperature of 65°F (18°C) in winter. In the right conditions it should flower twice a year.

Bougainvillea. Not often seen as a house plant, but if space allows for it to ramble up supports in a large room with a light airy position, it is a superb feature. Its flowers are insignificant but the brilliantly coloured pink bracts last all through the summer on *B. glabra* (5-8 feet) and *B. sanderiana*. It requires a minimum temperature of 55°F (13°C), plenty of water and feeding from spring to late autumn. Do not feed it after that until you cut back the previous year's growth to within 1 inch of its base in early spring.

Illustrated right: Begonia (above), Fuschia (below left) and Aphelandra squarrosa (below right)

flowering plants for autumn and winter

Senecio cruentus (Cineraria). All the varieties grown in pots have been derived from this one species and are superb winter-flowering house plants. The leaves are green on top but ash-coloured underneath, and the daisy-like flowers come in a multitude of brilliant colours, some single, others mixed. Most of the varieties grow about a foot high, and if you regularly remove dead flower heads and leaves the plants will remain attractive and bushy. Cool conditions, a light position and food and water while flowering are the main requirements. Discard after flowering.

Camellia. These are essentially hardy evergreen shrubs with shiny, dark green leaves, attractive single or double or striped flowers of white, pink or red, which make good house plants and require little attention. They grow 1-3 feet high in pots and flower through the dull winter months. Position in a light airy place and ensure the soil compost is kept evenly moist or the flower buds may fall. Sponge the leaves at intervals and keep the temperature at about 50°F (10°C). Remove dead heads and prune unwanted shoots after flowering. There are a mass of varieties to choose from and new ones are frequently introduced.

Chrysanthemum. Although these plants can now be produced in flower at any time of year, thanks to special growing techniques, people still regard them as autumn/winter plants. So complex has the formation of the flowers become that a botanical treatise would be required to explain them all.

Essentially among pot-grown 'Mums', the florist offers pompons (with smallish heads of flowers made of many curved petals), sprays — some times referred to as American sprays (with single, semi-single or double blooms up the stems at intervals), decoratives or 'mop heads', (with a mass of petals that form one large 'ball' flower per stem), quilled (with very fine petals), and cascades (which produce a mass of daisy-like flowers which literally pour over the side of a hanging basket or pot). With the exception of blue and black, Chrysanthemums can be obtained in virtually every shade of colour. Given a moderate temperature,

a light position, regular watering, feeding and removal of dead heads, they are one of the best long-lasting flowering plants for the home. Generally discarded after flowering, they can be planted in the garden but will not make good pot plants a second time. So many varieties are grown that it is impossible to keep pace with the names, and one usually buys unnamed plants from shops.

Calluna (Heather or Ling) and *Erica* (Heaths). Together these are generally referred to as Heather, and in overall appearance and necessary conditions for cultivation there is little variation. Both form shrubby evergreen plants with needle-like leaves in various shades of green or a beautiful golden-yellow copper and autumnal russet. The flowers are small and tubular and, because there are so many varieties, many colours abound, especially purple, pink, red and white — generally singly but sometimes as bi-colours. Few *Callunas* are successful pot plants; the *Ericas* adapt more readily to indoor conditions. For autumn and winter flowers try *E. gracilis* (1-1½ feet, rosy purple); *E. hyemalis* (Winter Heath, 1½ feet, pink-tinted white); *E. persoluta* (1-3 feet, soft red); and *E. carnea* (up to 1½ feet, in many shades). New varieties are introduced regularly and you may find all sorts in the shops. *Callunas* and *Ericas* should be grown in lime-free compost and watered regularly (with rainwater if possible) all year round to keep the compost evenly moist. They do not like over-heated dry rooms and it helps to place their pot in an outer container of moist peat. They rarely flower a second year, so throw away after flowering.

Polyanthus. In appearance Polyanthus are very similiar to Primulas (described under spring-flowering house plants) and require the same growing conditions indoors. Their brilliant flowers are eye-catching in winter when colour is important and the primrose-like leaves are almost swamped. One particularly attractive group are the gold-laced forms with narrow bands of golden-yellow round the edges of the flower petals. Other showy varieties are the Pacific, Festival and Giant

Bouquet strains, but usually the plants are grown from mixed seed and unnamed and you just choose your preferred colour and flower form. Put the plant in the garden after flowering or discard.

Begonia. Fibrous rooted Begonias that bloom in spring/early summer have been described earlier. In addition there are several autumn and winter varieties known as Christmas Begonias, which are raised from *B. Gloire de Lorraine*. Usually the flowers are red, but the blooms of *B. glaucophylla* are pink and pendulous, ideal for hanging baskets, *B. scharffianas* are white and *B. fuchsioides* and *B. froebellis* are scarlet. Culture and care are identical to what is needed for spring Begonias.

Capsicum (Christmas Pepper). The flowers are insignificant on these shrubby pot plants which are usually grown for their highly coloured spiky red fruits which last for a long period of the winter. A warmish room about 60°F (15.5°C)—and a light but not draughty position is required for healthy growth. The compost should be kept evenly moist and liquid fertilizer given every 10-14 days. Discard when leaves fall and fruits wither.

Solanum. This is a genus of numerous kinds of plants, most of them hardy enough for outdoor growing. There is one particularly popular for indoor colour in autumn and winter, *S. capsicastrum*, the Winter Cherry. It has unexciting flowers, but the bright orange-red fruits last for a long time and are very colourful. This small bushy plant should be kept in a coolish atmosphere, free from draughts and gas fumes, but it needs plenty of light. A moist atmosphere can be achieved by spraying the leaves and standing the pot in an outer container of moist peat in summer. After the berries have fallen stand the plant outdoors and cut back the stems to about 2 inches from the base. Sometimes (but unfortunately not always) this will encourage flowers and fruits for a second year.

Illustrated right: Camelia (above), Cineraria (below left) and a quilled Chrysanthemum (below right)

scented plants

'Flowers are not as fragrant as they used to be!' is a frequent complaint. Here is a selection which can be relied upon to fill a room with scent (a particularly lovely present for a blind person or an invalid). Treat them as you would any other flowering indoor plant.

Perhaps the first name that springs to mind is Jasmine, flower of many an Arabian Night's tale. Only some varieties are scented, however, so be sure to get the right kind. *Jasminum officinale* (the common Jasmine) has white flowers which smell particularly sweet in late summer, especially in the evening, and is suitable for indoor growing. Its long stems, covered in neat leaves and flowers, can be trained to grow 30 or 40 feet along a wall or shelves. If you wish to keep the plant more compact, prune the stems before the flowering season, or train them around wire hoops, canes or similiar supports. Other fragrant varieties, all white, are *J. gracillimum* (shorter and winter flowering), *J. sambac* (shorter, autumn-flowering and convenient since it does not shed its leaves), and *J. grandiflorum* (another long climber, flowering early in summer). All these are tropical varieties and so need a little warmth. *J. officinale* and *J. polyanthemum* will be happy in a cool room, as will the colourful *J. stephanense*, a climber which has pink flowers in the summer. At the end of winter, Jasmine needs a little pruning and tidying up and additional watering, preferably by spraying the foliage. The hardier varieties benefit from a spell outdoors during the summer.

Nip off shoots which have finished flowering. Cut off green shoots to start new plants: simply put them in pots of sandy compost.

Heliotropium, the Heliotrope, or Cherry Pie, is named after the sun (*helios*, Greek), which tells you what kind of conditions it likes. Compact and velvety, Heliotropes grow better if they are cut back to 2 inches-3 inches at the end of winter, and if their tops are pinched out when they are 5 inches tall

Illustrated left: Stephanotis with waxy, sweetly-scented flowers

to prevent them from becoming tall and straggly. Cuttings taken in autumn can be used to start new plants. Among the sweetly scented strains are *H. marine* (packed heads of violet-purple flowers), *H. peruvianum* and Lemoine's Giant.

Of all the *Gardenia* varieties, *G. jasminoides* is the one usually grown, producing its fragrant waxy, white flowers for weeks on end in summer and growing to a height of 2-6 feet. If you like double blooms, ask for the *florida* variety. Gardenias need plenty of warmth, water and sunshine. Prune and pinch back shoots to keep the plant shapely. As it ages it will cease to produce flowers.

The botanical name of the Oleander, or Rose-Bay, is *Nerium* from a Greek word meaning humid, and it needs to be watered and fed freely. It is an evergreen shrub on which magnificent clusters of graceful pink flowers appear early in summer. *N. oleander* can grow 6-10 feet high, and so is suitable for arrangements in a big tub or urn. Spraying the foliage helps these shrubs. Prune any new shoots back after flowering has finished, and reduce watering until growth starts again. Oleander leaves are extremely poisonous and planting is not advisable where children or pets live.

Hoya carnosa, the Honey Plant, is an evergreen climber which can grow 10-12 feet long, bearing clusters of waxy, sweetly scented, pink and white flowers in the summer. It need moder-

ate warmth, a sunny position and occasional thinning. But do not remove the bloom-stalks as a second crop of flowers will appear on them.

Another evergreen, the *Citrus sinensis* or Sweet Orange Tree, makes a decorative room plant — tall, with fragrant white blossom and, later on, little oranges. Do not confuse it with other orange-fruited indoor plants whose flowers lack scent. It may need quite a big tub, and it is advisable to prune it during the winter, and water and spray it well during summer.

Genista (Broom) is a familiar shrub outdoors: almost leafless, and smothered with small golden flowers. Varieties with a pleasing scent, like *G. cinerea* with its mass of summer blooms, are usually best grown indoors. Other fragrant varieties are *G. ephedroides* with small single flowers at the end of its stems in early summer; and *G. monosperma* with milky-white blooms. They need very little warmth, light pruning after the flowering has finished, and normal watering.

Stephanotis, a climber, has abundant clusters of waxy, white flowers. It is sometimes called Madagascar Jasmine because the fragrance is similiar to true Jasmine. The flowers appear sporadically throughout the year and are often used by florists in wedding bouquets. *Stephanotis* likes a warm room and, once growth starts, it needs proper training up strings or a frame-work of sticks, or it will twine itself into a tangle. Unwanted shoots should be cut off promptly, and the whole plant pruned drastically in early spring. Give fertilizer when watering and, if any pests appear, use a systemic insecticide. New plants can be produced from cuttings.

Exacum affine is a small plant well worth seeking out not only for its fragrance but because of the abundance of its neat and cheerful little flowers, bluish-lilac with yellow centres which continue for many months of the year. Although Exacums need shade and moisture, they should never be allowed to get too damp or too cold.

The world of bulbs opens up a whole new range of perfumed pleasure, from the heady sweetness of some Lilies, Hyacinths and Lilies-of-the-Valley through to the more delicate fragrance of many *Narcissi*, Begonias and *Muscari ambrosiacum*, one of the Grape Hyacinths.

Of course, foliage as well as flowers can give a room a pleasant smell. Two herbs with decorative as well as aromatic leaves are Thyme and Rosemary, well worth including in a group of pot

plants. Thyme remains a small neat shrub, rarely growing higher than one foot and easy to shape. *T. citriodorus* has lemon-scented foliage and pink or lilac flowers and there are many other attractive strains with variegated grey or golden foliage contrasting with flowers of white, pink, red, mauve or purple. *Rosemarinus*, too, comes in many varieties, of which the low-growing *R. lavandulaceus* is probably most suitable indoors. Its profuse blue flowers continue to bloom over a long period, and its leaves are particularly aromatic.

Several *Pelargoniums* (commonly called Geraniums), as well as true Geraniums, have scented leaves — some reminiscent of nutmeg, roses, apples, verbena, peppermint or orange. Among the most popular are the varieties which have a pronounced smell of lemons: these include *P. crispum*, *P. variegatum*, *P. graveolens* Mabel Grey and *P. fulgidum* Scarlet Unique. These varieties also produce flowers as an additional bonus and several have variegated leaves.

It would not be difficult, from the above selection alone, to fill a room with fragrance as well as colour. Then, through the window — if the sill has space for a plant trough — might waft the scents of still more sweet-smelling flowers, such as Stocks, clove-scented Pinks, Tobacco Plants, dwarf Sweet Peas, Nasturtiums and Honeysuckle, growing up from a carpet of Pennyroyal or miniature Mint.

Nerium oleander (single form)

Gardenia jasminoides (double form)

bulbs for year-round colour

Strictly speaking, some so-called bulbs are not bulbs at all, but corms, tubers or rhizomes. A true bulb is an underground swelling of the stem: a mass of leaf-scales within which a new stem and flower later form. A tuber, too, is an underground stem but is solid, not scaly, and able to send out roots from several places. A corm is also solid, but its roots descend from only one place. Rhizomes are creeping, swollen stems, often partly above ground.

Like most plants, after growth has started bulbs prefer a fairly even temperature, and in centrally heated homes this is ensured. Indoor bulbs provide flowers earlier than outdoor ones if the room is not too hot or dry. Because light is vital to all flowers, colours may be less brilliant indoors, so it is important to place the pots in the best light once growth has advanced.

The biggest bulbs are usually the best, because they contain more nutrients. Some bulbs are 'prepared' or 'forced'.

This means they have had a specialized heat treatment or a chilling in order to alter their normal time of development, so that it is possible to get bulbs (of certain flowers) to flower in other months of the year. The most common examples of this are Hyacinths, Narcissi and Tulips, and also some Crocuses, *Muscari armeniaecum* and one or two Scillas.

Planting

Bulbs already contain most of the nourishment the plant will need. Many will grow in fibre containing negligible nutriment, in water or even on pebbles but most need more than that. If they are to thrive, they should be put into John Innes Potting Compost No. 2. Of the ones shown in these pages, the following should be put in bulb fibre: *Crocus*, *Chionodoxa*, *Fritillaria*, *Galanthus*, Hyacinth, *Narcissus* (including Daffodil), Tulip. All the rest need compost.

Fibre tends to dry quickly so it is better in a plastic or china bowl rather than a porous one; this need not have a drainage hole. Soak the fibre before use. With compost, not only a drainage hole but crocks or charcoal in the bottom are important, for accumulated water can rot bulbs.

Do not mix different bulbs in one bowl; and, if making a group of, for instance, Hyacinths, choose varieties that come

into flower at the same time. Put in as many bulbs as possible, but not touching one another. The tips should normally just show above the top of the fibre or compost, which should come to $\frac{1}{2}$ inch below the top of the pot to allow space for watering. Smaller bulbs, such as Crocus, should be $\frac{1}{2}$ inch below the surface.

Care

The pots should then stay in a dark but airy place, with the compost or fibre kept damp, for many weeks — until shoots are 2 to 3 inches high.

The cooler the room they go into, the better. In a warm, dry atmosphere more frequent watering will be needed. There are no rules about how often to water: just inspect regularly to see whether watering is needed.

Some bulbs are better started off out of doors — a sill or a porch will do — otherwise they may be encouraged to make a lot of long spindly leaves quickly at the expense of the flowers later. This is true of *Eranthis*, *Chionodoxa*, *Fritillaria*, *Galanthus*, Iris, *Muscari*, *Ornithogalum*, miniature *Narcissi*, *Scilla*, *Vallota*.

When indoors, the pots should be turned round occasionally because, like many flowers, those of bulbs tend to strain towards the window. The nearer they are to daylight, the better — so long as strong sunlight does not scorch summer flowering ones.

Taller ones may need support, but use

Illustrated right:
Hyacinth, Crocus and Daffodils (above)
Chionodoxa gigantica (below left) and
Schizostylus coccinea major (below right)

Spring flowering bulbs — from left to right, Muscari botryoides (Grape Hyacinth),
Puschkina scilloides (Squills), Richardia aethiopica (Arum Lily)

sticks as slender and inconspicuous as possible.

Bulbs should not be thrown away after they have flowered. Continue watering (with liquid fertilizer added occasionally) until the leaves are completely dead, then store the bulbs in a paper bag, left open, to replant next year. When they start growing again, add a little liquid fertilizer to the water throughout the growing period.

The only exceptions to this are forced Tulips and Lilies-of-the-Valley, which will not flower a second time in pots but may do so, two years later, if planted in the meanwhile in the garden.

Spring Flowering Bulbs

Bulbs, for many people, are associated only with spring. In fact, they can provide colour all the year round. All the same, the spring favourites — *Narcissi* (including Daffodils) and Crocuses — will probably remain the most popular first choice.

There are many varieties of *Narcissi* and Daffodils which can be grown in pots and between them provide colour for nearly three months of the year. Florists sell many different types, usually when the plants are just in bud. The two varieties most commonly grown from bulbs planted in the autumn are the Paperwhites and Soleil d' Or, since they are particularly easy to start under home conditions. Keep pots of Narcissi (at least 3 bulbs to a pot) cool, dark and slightly damp until the shoots are 4 inches high and the flower buds well in view. If the flower buds stay hidden, remove the side

shoots when transferring the pot to a warmer room. Spray the buds lightly until they have opened.

Crocuses provide a bewildering choice of brilliant colours. The two-colour varieties form a particularly decorative group. Vernus Violet Vanguard blooms very early when other flowers are few. Its colouring is particularly charming: a pretty blue with delicate French grey outside. It is just one of the many large-flowered varieties (height about 4 inches) but there are smaller species which are particularly effective planted close together in a large bowl or crocus dish (a special pot with holes in the sides as well as at the top in which to plant bulbs so that when they flower the Crocuses form a colourful 'mound'). Another dimunitive flower which gives a welcome splash of colour as soon as winter is over is *Chionodoxa*, Glory-of-the-Snow. One of its most elegant varieties, *C. gigantea*, has enormous flowers of a pale violet with an ice-blue centre. Plant the little bulbs in a group. Other attractive ones are *C. lucilea rosea*, with pink blooms, and the lovely deep gentian-blue *C. sardensis*.

The *Schizostylis coccinea* or Kaffir Lily, which is not a true lily at all, is a striking bulb for spring flowering. It grows up to 3 feet tall and bears a graceful spike of about a dozen red or pink flowers.

Other bulbs to plant for spring bloom-

ing include: *Muscari* (Grape Hyacinths), *Puschkinia scilloides* (Squills) and *Scillas*. All of these are small and blue. The starry little *Sparaxis* and *Ornithogalum* are also small, and the former is available in many colours, while the latter is usually white. Among taller plants, many of the *Allium* family flower early in the year (with big globular heads of little flowerets), and there is a choice among Irises, Lilies and Fritillarias. Be sure to select varieties suitable for growing indoors. *Richardia* (Arum Lily) and *Ixia* (African Corn Lily) are even more spectacular where there is space to show them off well.

Summer Flowering Bulbs

When summer comes, there is almost an embarrassment of riches, particularly among the *Lilium* (Lilies), many of which give scent as well as colour to a room. One of the tallest and most handsome of plants grown from bulbs, the Lily gives excellent value for money because its flowers are long-lasting. Lilies need deep pots, and are at their best in a group of three. The *auratum* variety (Queen of Lilies) is particularly recommended for growing in pots: huge waxy flowers, several to a stem, are deeply scented and often decorated with distinctive golden stripes and crimson spots. They grow with great vigour and need little care. *L. speciosum* (crimson markings on cream petals) and its varieties in white, red or pink,

Illustrated right: Agapanthus africanus (above), Amaryllis (below left) and Solomon's Seal (below right)

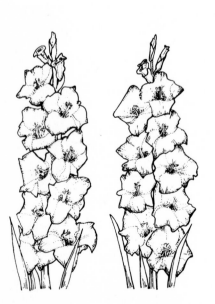

Summer flowering bulbs — from left to right, Gladiolus (Sword Lily), Achimenes (Hot Water Plant), Valotta speciosa (The Scarborough Lily)

and *L.longiflorum* and its varieties, with white funnel-shaped flowers, are also popular and particularly suitable for pot growing.

Another lily-like flower, easy to grow and deserving a pot to itself, is *Amaryllis belladonna* (Belladonna Lily), which produces several enormous fragrant pink or deep red flowers. The *Amaryllis* is frequently confused with the *Hippeastrum* as they look very similar. There are many species and varieties suitable for pot growing. Flower colours vary considerably; some are bi-coloured at the top of a $1\frac{1}{2}$-2 foot stem.

Agapanthus, too, is spectacular, particularly if a group can be grown in one large tub or urn. Sometimes called African Lilies, they have round heads consisting of dozens of small flowers. The best-known variety, *A.umbellatus*, grows 2-3 feet tall with bright blue or white flowers. *Agapanthus* needs plenty of water and fertilizer during summer.

For a more discreet charm, a group of *Polygonatum* (Solomon's Seal) could grace the corner of a cool room, perhaps among Ferns. *P.multiflorum* is the best choice for growing in a pot: from each arching stem hangs a row of small greenish-white bells.

Other well-known bulbs for summer include a few varieties of *Gladioli*, tuberous *Begonia* and *Montbretia*. If you want to try something less familiar, look for *Brodiaea uniflora* (profuse, neat flowers on 6 inch stems, which remain in bloom a long time and smell sweetly), *Tritonia crocata* (taller, with long-lasting, funnel-shaped, orange flowers), *Streptanthera cuprea coccinae* (exotic orange and black flowers borne on 9-inch stems among a fan of sword-shaped leaves), *Achimenes* (the small, prettily drooping magenta or pink flowers last a long time and the plants multiply every year — a good choice for hanging baskets), *Crinum powellii* (the Cape Lily — handsome white, lily-like flowers veined with red), and *Valotta specioza* (at least 18 inches high with several funnel-shaped flowers in bright scarlet).

Autumn/Winter Flowering Bulbs

As the year wears on and cut flowers become expensive, bulbs which bloom during autumn are particularly useful around the house. There are several varieties of Lily and Crocus which flower in the autumn, as well as Hyacinths and Tulips. Some specially forced to bloom during the coldest weather give a wonderful glow of colour during the winter.

Autumn is also the time when Cyclamens come into their own, along with *Colchicums* (sometimes called Naked Boys because their crocus-like flowers first appear without any leaves), *Liriopes* (small spires of deep purple flowers followed by blue-black berries), little *Sternbergias* (golden star-like flowers that grow in groups), *Zephryanthes candida* (white and crocus-like) and the strange *Sauromatum guttata* (Monarch-of-the-East), which, without either soil or water, soon produces on a stem nearly 2 feet tall a green and purple-spotted leaf-like flower with a rather unpleasant smell.

Winter's most enchanting flower is perhaps the *Galanthus* (Snowdrop), its drooping white head delicately touched with green. There are doubles, giants and some with outward-curving petals. The *Nerine*, by contrast, is a brilliant and spectacular plant: on 18-inch stems large round heads of lily-like pink flowers, sometimes gold-flecked, appear.

In winter, slender multi-coloured Freesias give a touch of gaiety and *Convallaria* (Lilies-of-the-Valley) their sweet perfume. *Eranthis hyemalis* (Winter Aconites), similar to Buttercups, or *Lachenalia* (Cape Cowslips) can be planted in a clump to give a sunny splash of colour. There is a pendulous variety of the latter, (*L. pendula*), which would be ideal for a hanging basket. Its flowers are red, edged with green and purple.

Bulbs, in short, can be found for any month of the year and for any purpose: to fill a large alcove with one tall and striking splash of colour, to hang gracefully from a basket or wall-container, or to decorate the corner of a desk with a cluster of miniature blooms near eye-level. Chain-stores offer a good choice of bulbs these days, and there are many specialists whose mail-order catalogues offer a feast of all that is best or rarest. Bulbs are, perhaps, the easiest kind of plant for the indoor gardener to obtain — and to grow.

Illustrated right: Snowdrop (above), Greigii Tulip (below left) Nerine (below right)

Autumn/Winter flowering bulbs — from left to right, Freesia refracta, Convallaria (Lily of the Valley), Colchicum autumnale (Naked Boys)

orchids

To many people Orchids are the finest of all plants. There are some that can be grown in the home as pot plants without much difficulty, provided each is given individual care and attention. An Orchid may be bought already in flower at various times of the year, but it is preferable to get it in the spring so that it has time to settle in its new home during the summer months. It is also advisable to buy a mature plant rather than a seedling, even if it is more expensive, as the results are likely to be much more satisfactory.

Initially you should be able to keep your new Orchid in flower for several weeks if you treat it correctly right from the start. It should then produce a fresh crop of flowers regularly each successive year. In general, Orchids like a light but not sunny position and one which is draught-free — though they need plenty of ventilation, provided it is not an icy blast. (Orchids preferring shady spots include the *Paphiopedilums* and *Masdevallias*.) A round-the-year temperature of around 60°F (16°C) is about right for most varieties, though they can well stand a few degrees higher or lower.

Like many plants, Orchids have a growing season and a resting period each year. During their growing period, in order to help give them the conditions they like best, each pot should be stood on a tray or shallow container with a 2 inch layer of gravel or pebbles at the bottom. Water should be poured over this layer to a depth of 1 inch. In this way the plants have a moist atmosphere, but the base of the pot and the plant's roots are not in direct contact with the water. The 1 inch of water in the tray should be kept topped up, and occasionally the tray and gravel or pebbles should be washed to ensure clean growing conditions.

During the resting period of the Orchid, the pot can be stood in a dry container — just something to catch any surplus water drips. When the plants are growing well and freely, water the compost thoroughly whenever it appears to be drying out; also spray the plants from time to time. During the resting period, however, when the Orchids are making little growth, water them sparingly — just enough to prevent the compost from drying out completely. If possible always use soft water like rain water, at room temperature.

The less you re-pot Orchids the better. However, it will probably become necessary every other year and should be done just when the plants are starting to grow again after their resting period. For re-potting, buy special Orchid compost containing a lot of peat, sphagnum moss and charcoal; alternatively, get Osmunda fibre and mix three parts of that with one part of sphagnum moss. This is a particularly good mixture because the Orchids feed on the Osmunda as it breaks down.

Most Orchids require little artificial

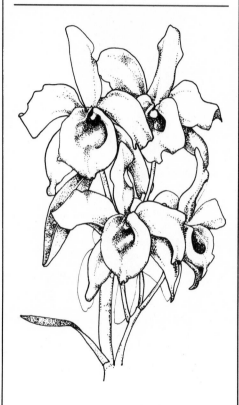

Dendrobium nobile has many different forms, and comes originally from the Far East

feeding but they do benefit from a very weak solution of liquid fertilizer in the water during their growing period. When re-potting, fill the pot one third full of crocks before putting the compost in. Then remove the orchid from its pot, cut off any brown roots or bulbs, and plant it firmly but gently in its new container. As many Orchids are epiphytes (plants which grow on trees and feed by aerial roots), do not be surprised to find roots growing above the compost.

If your Orchids get too big and you want to divide them up into smaller plants, simply separate the bulbs or plants when they are not in flower but growing freely and keep the new ones in a warm, moist place until they are growing freely again.

There are quite a number of Orchids which can be grown in the home and one of the easiest is *Cypripedium insigne* (Lady's Slipper), with flowers that really look like slippers in brown, yellow and green and are waxy and speckled. This Orchid's natural habitat is N.W. India. It is completely untemperamental and requires no particular culture. It is equally indifferent to overwatering and underwatering and flowers regularly each year.

Another Orchid which grows happily indoors is *Epidendrum vitellinum* (small, single, scarlet). Its natural habitat is Mexico, where it grows at high altitudes in the tops of trees. A great favourite in Victorian greenhouses, it is not often seen today but it deserves a place in any collection of pot plants. The scarlet flowers appear each year and last for about six weeks on the plant. Another easy to grow Orchid is *Odontoglossum* and its hybrids. The species comes from Central America but the hybridizing has been done in Britain. It was popular early in this century as a button-hole flower for the well-dressed man. Now it is grown rather for its lack of any particular flowering season, so that a well selected group of plants will provide flowers all the year round.

Other recommended orchids are:
Coelogyne cristata (snow-white with yellow lip) and its varieties
Dendrobium nobile varieties (white and rose)
Laelia anceps (pinky red spikes)
Lycaste skinneri (single flowers of pink and white)
Maxillaria picta (creamy-yellow dotted brown)
Odontoglossum grande (orange-yellow and brown) and other varieties
Paphiopedilum insigne (very variable — greenish-brown, white or purple spotted)
Cymbidium eburneum (white).

If you become an Orchid enthusiast, one of the simplest ways is to grow a collection of plants which all require the same type of treatment and care in either Ward cases or heated propagating cases with raised domes.

Illustrated right: Cypripedium insigne (Slipper orchid) at the left, Odontoglossum hybrid in the centre and Epidendrum vitellinum shown right — three varieties that require the minimum amount of care and attention to grow successfully indoors

pips and stones

Plants grown from the pips and stones of fruit native to warm climates can be cultivated in a cool climate, provided you have central heating or even a cupboard with a hot tank in it.

Peaches, apricots, nectarines

First, crack the stone a little — just enough to break the sides open slightly. Then plant it in a 4 inch pot of compost, about 1 inch deep. Put the pot in a warm, shady place and keep the compost damp. After some months, a little shoot should appear. Place the pot in a sunny position. Each spring, cut back the branches to a compact shape. A spell outdoors in the sun every summer will help, and so will liquid fertilizer when watering. Re-pot when the plant grows bigger. You may get flowers, but fruit is unlikely.

Avocados for giant plants

An Avocado stone needs to be started off in the dark. It can be grown in compost, but it is easier and more interesting to put it first (small end up) in a narrow glass with water reaching half way up: you will be able to watch the initial root and shoot growth. Foil around the glass will keep light out but won't exclude air.

Put the glass near a radiator or hot tank and keep the water topped up. If the stone gets slimy, rinse it under the tap and put it back in clean water. The stone should start to split within a month or two, and a root and shoot will appear from it. When these are an inch long, the stone should go into a 6 inch pot of compost. Keep it out of strong light until it is 3 inches tall. In years to come it will grow several feet high if it gets enough sunshine and protection from draughts. A stick for support and, in due course, a bigger pot are likely to be needed. Regular watering (with liquid fertilizer added) is necessary.

Avocados at varying stages of growth. The stone that is just beginning to split should be kept in a dark warm place. The stone on the left shows the stage at which the plant can emerge into the light to be planted in compost

Trees from citrus pips

The pips of Oranges, Lemons, Grape-fruits or (prettiest of all) Tangerines are best planted in spring. Put three pips of one kind in each 3-inch pot of damp compost, about ½ inch down, or plant in fruit skin halves.

As with Avocado stones, darkness and warmth are needed, and regular checks on the dampness of the compost. When shoots appear a month or two later, gradually bring the plant nearer full light and when it is 4 inches tall transfer it to a bigger pot of compost. An advantage of growing pips in fruit skins is that the skin too can be planted, thus avoiding any disturbance of the roots: they will grow through the skin. A few months later, there should be the beginnings of a small, glossy-leaved tree which in years to come might even produce flowers and fruit. Care for it like a Peach tree (see above). Citrus pips can be used to grow a forest in a dish. Collect dozens of pips, soak overnight, press down all over damp compost and sprinkle a little more of it on top. Keep damp, adding a little liquid fertilizer to the water, and in a few weeks a glossy-leaved, miniature forest will fill the dish.

Palms from date stones

These are trickier because they come from a very hot climate. Plant several to a pot like citrus pips (see above)

Orange tree

and put the pot right on a radiator or hot tank, covered with a polythene bag to keep draughts out and moisture in. When shoots appear, use small sticks to prop up the bag so that it does not touch them. When the plants are 3 inches high, you can remove the bag but they must be kept warm and regularly given water containing liquid fertilizer.

Fast results from mangoes and lychees

Both these fruits have stones which can produce impressive plants swiftly once they have germinated.

Start them off in the same way as Avocados (see above). It will be two or three months before growth starts but then it will be rapid. The Lychee can grow 6 feet of leafy stem in a year; the Mango produces extraordinary contortions of stem initially and then lovely long leaves. Both need plentiful moisture as well as warmth. The steam of a bathroom is ideal, provided the room remains fairly warm at night.

Creepers from melons, marrows and cucumbers

These grow quickly from pips if started off in spring in the same way as citrus pips (see above), but with warmth throughout their life. Small plants should have grown within a month or two, with 4 foot creepers by the end of the year. These will need strings or wires fixed to a wall to which to cling. You may even get edible fruits if you cross-pollinate the flowers of each plant, by dabbing them with cotton-wool.

Apple, pear and plum trees

No great heat is needed for these. In fact, the reverse is true. Start by placing pips or stones between pads of cotton-wool (which must be kept moist) in the refrigerator until shoots appear. Then plant in compost and treat in the usual way. (Cherry stones can be treated like this, too, but are less reliable.)

Nuts

Walnuts and Hazels may grow into little trees if you plant them in sand in late autumn, leave in a cool and dark place, then carefully transplant to compost in spring. An acorn can be suspended on a string in water, or (like other seeds from trees) planted in compost.

decorative vegetable tops

One of the pleasures of childhood was growing Carrot tops in saucers.

The decorative results of the simple technique make it worth including in the adult's repertoire of indoor gardening. And there are other treasures that deserve, like the Carrot tops, to be saved from a fate in the garbage can.

Carrots, turnips, parsnips, beets, swedes, radishes

Provided these root vegetables are not of a packaged kind that has been frozen before reaching the shop (nor — in the case of beets — cooked), nothing is easier than producing foliage from a ½-inch slice off the top of any of them. Stand the slice in a saucer with just enough water to cover the bottom part, and put in a light place. Keep the bottom moist. If the weather is fairly warm, leaf shoots will appear within days, and leaves after a week or two. They will be feathery ones, in the case of Carrots; and green with red veins in the case of Beets and Turnips.

Hanging carrots and parsnips

You can grow these upside down — in mid-air. A 2-inch slice from the top is needed. Scoop out 1 inch of the core from the cut end. The point of a potato peeler is handy for this, but don't pierce the sides with it. Stick a skewer through from one side to the other, near the cut end, and thread wire through by which to hang the vegetable up like a small basket. If the hollow is kept filled with water and the vegetable hangs in a light and warm place, leaves will soon sprout from the bottom and start to grow upwards.

Another plant could be grown in the 'basket' at the same time if it has moist compost in it. You could also plant a seed or two of some tiny plant such as dwarf Nasturtium.

A potato creeper

This one, which should be started in spring, needs a jar of water and a card with a hole in the middle on which to perch the Potato. This should have as many 'eyes' as possible at the top, and be half submerged in the water. It is therefore important to keep topping up the water and to change it if it gets smelly.

Leave the jar in a cool, dark place until roots appear. When shoots grow, cut off all but two. These should grow up to six feet long during the summer, provided the plant gets light and some warmth. A little liquid fertilizer can be added to the water to help. Fasten strings or wires up a wall or window frame, and tie the climbing shoots to them.

Baby Potatoes will probably form on the roots, but they will not be edible unless you keep the light from them. A small bit of Potato, provided it has some 'eyes', will also produce a creeper (though a smaller one) if grown in a saucer like a carrot top.

Sweet Potatoes can be treated in the same way.

Mint and watercress

Just below one pair of leaves, snip off the top of a sprig and put it in a jar of water in a light place. It will form roots and produce a new plant.

Onions

These tend to sprout of their own accord. With encouragement, they will produce handsome (if smelly) flowers. Plant like a bulb in compost. The pot should be 6 inches deep, the Onion only half buried, and the compost kept damp. An Onion planted in early spring and kept in a light place should, during summer, grow about 1½ feet tall with a big globe of mauve flowers. It will probably need a stick for support. After flowering, the flower head can be hung upside down to dry and its seeds used next spring in a garden or window box.

Beans and peas in jars

Line a jam jar with damp blotting or other absorbent paper and slip some Broad Beans (or Peas) between it and the glass, near the top. The 'scars' on the sides of the beans should be vertical. Keep enough water in the jar to ensure that the paper is always damp. After a few days, the skin of each bean will crack and a root appear, followed by a shoot. When the shoots are about 3 inches high, they will need more than just water to feed on: add a little liquid fertilizer to the water. With luck you should get some flowers, though bean pods are not likely to grow. (Dried cooking beans may be too dry: buy packet seeds.)

Pineapple tops

These (which belong to the Bromeliad family) have been known to grow well in saucers like Carrots for a while. They do better still if transferred to a 6-inch pot of sand with a polythene bag over the top of the pot at first. Pineapple tops are more likely to root well if you have chosen a fruit with really healthy leaves. Having cut the top inch off the pineapple, leave it on its side for a day or two to dry before planting.

Warmth, light and water (with liquid fertilizer added to it) are needed, of course. Trickle the water into the top of the plant for the first two weeks; after that, water the sand round it.

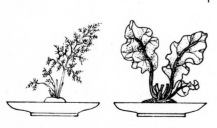    

Growing carrot, beetroot, parsnip and turnip tops, a potato creeper and watercress

miniature gardens

Any shallow container, from a soup plate upwards, could be used for this. Even baskets or wood boxes will do if lined with plastic or a double thickness of cooking foil. If, as is likely, the container does not have any drainage holes, then a 1-inch layer of pebbles or charcoal should go in before filling with John Innes Compost No. 2, well moistened, to ½ inch below the top.

The choice of plants should be determined first by where you are going to stand the garden (in light or shade, with or without central heating, and so on), second by their watering needs (don't mix cacti with plants that need more water) and finally by their growth (some plants which are tiny to start with can leap ahead and dominate the rest).

Low, trailing plants are an obvious choice for the front of the garden, with taller ones further back — perhaps even a little Bonsai tree. The effect is improved if the compost is heaped up a bit towards the back, and a few pebbles or small rocks added. Some people enjoy modelling bridges or urns, making pools from pieces of mirror, adding sea shells, toy birds, paths of sand, and so forth. Covering the surface with gravel or aquarium chips is a good idea, not merely for appearance but to reduce the evaporation of moisture from the compost. Water loss is a particular problem with these gardens, which have a large surface area. A big plastic bag can be put over the whole container at times, and spraying the leaves is a help. Grass grown from seed and trimmed with scissors will help to conserve moisture.

In choosing plants, try to vary the shapes of the plants and of their leaves and pick contrasting foliage colours. Use your finger or a teaspoon to dig holes large enough to take the plant's roots without crushing them in. Press the compost down firmly.

A garden like this is best started in spring or early summer, watered adequately (with liquid fertilizer added to the water) throughout the growing and flowering months, then fairly drastically thinned out in autumn. Some plants may by then need digging up and dividing in two, or at least cutting back. As with most indoor plants, they appreciate a spell outdoors during summer, but not standing in the full blaze of sun.

Here are some suggestions for plant combinations:

Long-lasting flowers in brilliant pinks and reds are produced by Centaury and Pimpernel if stood in a sunny spot. The former, 2 to 3 inches high, has glossy leaves; the latter is a very low plant, ideal for overhanging the edges of the container. For contrast, add a white miniature Rose (6 to 10 inches high) at the back and a small variety of Pelargonium or a Busy Lizzie cut back regularly to the required size. Keep out of direct sunlight and well watered.

A group of succulents needing very little watering: Cacti are an obvious choice or a collection of Saxifrages of different varieties, green and silvery. They will spread and mingle with one another. The Saxifrages should be kept in light shade. Succulents that can be kept small if not given too much compost include *Aloe*, *Crassula*, *Sempervivum*, *Kalenchoe*, *Sedum* and *Kleinia*. If you choose varieties of different heights these plants can make a very decorative all-year display, needing little attention.

A demure pink and white garden to put where there is no sun (but adequate light) might have in it *Viola hederacea* (Australian Violets) which are white with purple splashes, *Crassula bolusii* or *cooperi* — pink flowers above rosettes of pale green leaves, red on their under-sides, and another variety of Pimpernel — *Anagallis collina* — which is pink and shade-loving. With them could go a dwarf Cypress or Juniper tree at the back, if the garden gets enough light. As the *Crassula* needs less watering than the rest, plant it in its own separate pot so that water applied to the others will pass it by.

A miniature bulb garden would be enchanting. You might choose small spring bulbs like indoor Crocuses and Snowdrops for a yellow and white scheme, or Grape hyacinths or *Chionodoxa* (Glory-of-the-Snow) for their beautiful blue. Add *Helxine soleirolii aurea* (Baby's Tears) for an all-over carpet of tiny golden leaves brimming over the edges of the container through which the bulbs can thrust their shoots later. Do not over water.

An attractive grouping of foliage plants with coloured leaf-markings could consist of *Tradescantia*, *Pilea cadierei* and *Pilea Moon Valley*, *Nidularium* (Bird's Nest Bromeliad), *Scindapsis Marble Queen*, *Fittonia*, *Peperomia*, *Saxifraga sarmentosum* and *Zebrina*.

Miniature garden around a Bonsai tree   *Succulents grouped together*   *A miniature garden of spring bulbs*

bottle gardens

These are both popular and amusing. All you need for a bottle garden is a very large bottle, jar or carboy. Fill it 6-8 inches deep with a good potting compost to which you have added a little charcoal. It is a good idea to pour the dry soil in through a funnel as the sides of the vessel should not be covered in soil. (Damp soil will not pour in easily and may stick to the sides.)

Your plants will have to be inserted with the help of sticks on which spoons or trowels are tied. Make sure the plants are small as this is a delicate operation.

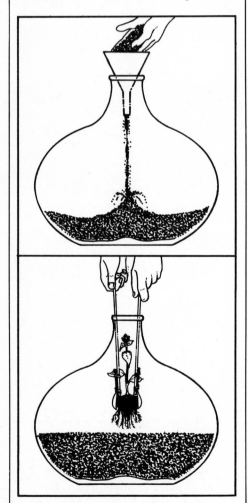

Cover the plant roots with soil as well as you can by jiggling the spoons about. If you are not very successful at this do not worry—the plants will root themselves when they have been watered. When you have put in all the plants water them by dribbling the water down the sides of the bottle.

It is not necessary to water a bottle garden as often as a pot plant, because a lot of air cannot get in, and the plants make their own climate. And if the bottle is corked or stoppered it will only require watering about once a year. It will, in effect, be self-watering—moisture given off by the leaves condensing on the side of the bottle and dripping back down to water the roots.

Stand your bottle garden in a good light but not in direct sunlight or the glass will get too hot.

Good plants for bottle gardens are those which are slow growing—*Peperomia*, *Maranta* (Prayer Plant), *Zebrina* and *Tradescantia* (Wandering Sailor), and *Pilea* (Aluminium Plant). These all have particularly decorative leaves.

Dead leaves and other undesirable materials are removed by cutting them off with a piece of razor-blade wired to a cane; they can then be lifted out on a pointed cane. The amount of debris which collects in the bottle will be kept to a minimum provided you choose suitable plants. Exactly the same principles, with less fuss, can be applied if you want to plant a large goldfish bowl, brandy glass, wide-necked jar, or a pan which can be covered with a bell glass.

wardian cases

An early Victorian botanist called Ward discovered that some plants grow happily in closed glass cases like tanks. Bottle gardens thrive on the same principle. Within such a case, the air is still and draught-free, uncontaminated by dust or other pollution, and as consistently dry or damp as required. The temperature does not fluctuate much and water is not lost through evaporation. Therefore many delicate plants, which would be hard to keep in the open, prosper inside with little, if any, attention.

Such cases can be small or large, kept indoors in a warm place or outdoors in the cool — and contain plants chosen accordingly.

As there are no drainage holes in such a container, a layer of charcoal at the bottom is needed and then a layer of peat. The compost (John Innes No. 2) looks best if not spread level but with some mounds, and a few stones or small rocks added. The plants should be grouped, with taller ones at the back and the smallest in front, but with space for growth between them. Moss can be added to cover the bare patches of compost.

The case should be kept in a light but not sunny position. Some ferns and ivies prefer shade. No watering should be needed, and no fertilizer. You will see water from the plants condensing occasionally on the glass and running back into the compost.

A glazier could provide you with glass with which to make your own Wardian case on a wooden frame, with a glass lid, or you could convert an aquarium tank. Garden shops now sell Perspex and polythene versions, intended as propagators for seedlings. If you can pick up from a junk shop an old Victorian glass dome (once used for covering stuffed birds, or over clocks) and find a bowl of matching size to put it on, you could grow one or two taller plants in this.

In addition, you could devote one case entirely to cacti, mixing sand with the compost. Another would do for ferns, ivies and other plants collected from a woodland. You might keep one case for fruit-pip plants, another for herbs or small flowering indoor plants. Do not mix plants that have different cultural needs. In the case of flowering plants, you will have to water very occasionally, ventilate if there is too much condensation, and remove dead flowers.

Wardian case with the tallest plants grouped at the back and the smaller ones in front

bonsai

The art of growing miniature trees, which rarely exceed two feet in height, is a living art form.

The Chinese and Indians are reputed to have grown miniature trees in the eighth century A.D., but by the tenth century the Japanese had taken up and developed the idea. 'Bonsai' is, in fact, a Japanese word meaning 'trees growing in shallow containers'.

Bonsai are kept small by pruning and by keeping them in a small container which restricts their root growth. Those grown over two feet are usually left outdoors, those 1-2 feet high stand alone indoors and those less than one foot high are often grouped—two or more growing in one container.

This beautiful mature bonsai is a particularly good one because its leaves and berries are in proportion with its size.
Two rocks give a grouping of Cypress bonsai the impression of a natural, rugged landscape (below).

One of the traditions of grouped bonsai is that an uneven number of trees is usually grown. This is because the Japanese regard uneven numbers as representative of longevity. A group of four trees is never grown, as the word four in Japanese is similar to the word for death.

Which trees to choose

In general the slow-growing or small trees are best for bonsai, as you then have less of a struggle against nature. (Slow trees can take 50 years to reach 20 feet, whereas fast-growing ones can exceed 100 feet in the same time.) Evergreens are popular and vary little from season to season, but you can also grow flowering and fruit trees. (Choose those that have small fruit—crab apple as against eating apple.) The trees should have small leaves, or short needles, which do not detract from the perfect, miniature look of the tree. The leaves will be small on bonsai because of the

pruning and dwarfing process but, again, if you choose a small-leaved tree you will have a head start.

Many types of tree not usually regarded as bonsai can be successfully grown in miniature form, so if you see anything that looks suitable it is worth attempting to grow it. But first find out as much as possible about the habits and soil preferences of the tree—the more you know about it the greater your chance of growing it successfully as a bonsai. Below are listed some of the more popular bonsai. They are all reasonably hardy and easy to keep alive.

Abies (Conifer). This exceptionally beautiful evergreen has short needles and a trunk which is wide at the base but tapers sharply.

Acer. The deciduous Acer family includes *Acer Palmatum* (Maple) and *Acer Pseudo-platanus* (Sycamore) which both have attractive leaves.

Betula (Birch). A graceful deciduous tree with small foliage and white or silver bark.

Chamaecyparis (False Cypress). An evergreen which is obtainable in various forms, and has very small leaves.

Cornus Mas (Cornelian Cherry). A deciduous tree which has small yellow clusters of flowers in early spring and edible red oval fruit later.

Cotoneaster. The many varieties of this tree—both deciduous and evergreen—have small leaves, flowers and fruit.

Fagus (Beech). This deciduous tree has a well-shaped trunk and pale green leaves in spring. The leaves turn to russet in autumn but stay on the tree throughout the winter.

Juniperus Communis (Juniper). A very small-leaved evergreen.

Lycium (Boxthorn). A deciduous tree with small purple flowers and red berries.

Malus (Crab Apple). A number of varieties of this deciduous tree are suitable for bonsai. It has small red or white blooms in early summer and small colourful fruit in autumn.

Morus Alba (Silkworm Mulberry). With its many small flowers and dark green leaves the form of this deciduous tree is particularly good.

Picea Abies (Spruce). A shallow-rooted evergreen with fine-needled foliage.

Pinus (Pine). The most popular of the bonsai and the Japanese symbol of life.

Prunus. The deciduous *Prunus* family includes the *Prunus Mume* (Apricot), *Prunus Jamasakura* (Cherry)—which dislikes pruning, and *Prunus Communis* (Almond). The Apricot is perhaps the easiest to grow. Choose a small-leaved and small-flowered variety.

Pyracantha Coccinea (Firethorn). A deciduous tree which has small leaves, and tiny white flowers in mid-summer. These turn to yellow or red berries in autumn, and last for about five months.

Quercus (Oak). Another deciduous tree, oak is particularly good for bonsai as it is slow growing and has lots of branches.

Salix (Willow). A deciduous tree, *Salix Babylonica* (the Weeping Willow) is particularly lovely.

Taxus (Yew). A hardy evergreen whose trunk naturally looks gnarled as the tree grows. It also produces attractive scarlet berries.

Tilia x Europaea (Lime). This lovely deciduous tree has red twigs, and small, pale green, heart-shaped leaves.

To buy or to grow?

There are basically two ways of obtaining a bonsai—either you buy it or you grow it. If you buy one you lose some of the absorbing work of pruning it and determining its shape, but you do see a mature end result.

You can buy one fully grown, container and all, from a specialist nursery. Or—from autumn to spring when they are resting—you can buy one grown but 'root-wrapped' (that is, with its ball of soil protectively wrapped in some way) rather than in a container. You then plant it yourself, which means you have the choice of container.

Alternatively, as bonsai are usually rather expensive to buy, you could grow your own from a seed, seedling or cutting. Oak, Willow, Beech, Sycamore, and Conifers are easy to grow in this way if you give them enough warmth, moisture and air.

The drawback here is that it can take up

to 100 years to develop a mature bonsai!

The major points to look for when buying or growing a bonsai are that the plant is small and attractive, that the trunk is thick in proportion to the height, that the plant itself and its roots look healthy, and that it has small leaves.

How to grow bonsai

An Acorn or Chestnut will grow if you plant it. You can take a cutting from a tree. Or, if you are lucky, you may find a suitable seedling. Cuttings should be 3 inches long, cut just below a leaf node so that they can drink easily. Take soft wood cuttings in the spring, and hard wood ones in autumn choosing wood of that year's growth.

To plant, make holes in the side and bottom of a pot (if it is clay you will need to drill these, if plastic you can make them using a sharp knife). Put crocks and gravel at the bottom of the pot to help drainage, then fill the pot with a sandy compost. A seed should be planted about its own height below the soil, a cutting about one third of its length, and a seedling as a plant. Leave half an inch at the top of the pot for watering.

As roots come through the holes in the pot snip them off, and after one year in the pot if it is a cutting or seedling, or two or three years for a seed, repot into its new container and, later, start pruning the top growth very carefully.

Watering

Water bonsai about once a day, never allow the soil to dry out, but be careful not to overwater. The soil should be kept just moist at all times.

You will need to water more frequently in hot weather and in the growing season and less in winter.

The larger leafed varieties of bonsai should have their leaves sprayed occasionally. But never do this in the heat of the day or while the tree is receiving direct sunlight. Sun on water droplets has the same effect as a magnifying glass—the leaves will be burnt or scorched.

Soil

Use different grades of coarse mixed soil which are suitable for your particular tree, some water retentive and some open and porous. If you use too fine a soil it will clog down when watered and not enough air will be able to circulate around the roots.

Put the coarsest soil in the bottom of

the pot, above the crocks, and the finest soil on top and around the roots.

Feeding

Bonsai, like pot plants, need regular feeding with a liquid fertilizer during the growing season. This is because their roots are restricted as to the area they can stretch out to in search of food.

Re-potting

This is best done in the dormant season when the plant is not growing. So, re-pot spring-flowering trees in autumn, deciduous trees in autumn or early spring, and conifers any time except midsummer and mid-winter.

Young trees, obviously, need repotting more frequently than old ones as they grow more quickly. To see if a tree needs repotting look at the bottom drainage holes, if more than two or three roots are poking out then it needs repotting. (If, on the other hand, none are visible some time after repotting check the plant, it is a sign that the roots are unhealthy.)

Let the soil dry out before repotting to make it easier to remove. Loosen the soil from around the roots, then repot with dry soil as this will not clog and prevent air circulating around the roots. Water well, and then leave the tree in a protected place—in the garden if there is no danger of frost—for a few days to recover and settle in.

Root pruning

This is done when repotting and does not, in itself, dwarf a tree—rather it promotes healthy growth. The fine roots feed the tree and the larger ones hold it firmly in the ground. Carefully knock off most of the earth, then trim the large coarse roots as, clearly, they are not really necessary to bonsai. Also remove any broken and dead roots. There should be a space of ¾-1 inch between the root ball and the side of the container.

Pruning roots in this way also helps to ensure that they get enough air. Too many roots tangled together (or heavy soil) prevent this. Remember to use a sharp tool when pruning the roots to avoid damaging or bruising them.

Wiring

Wire is twisted around the trunk or branches of bonsai to encourage growth in a particular direction, or to develop a gnarled-looking twist. Do not wire immediately following repotting as you

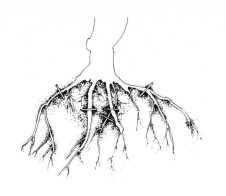

These roots should be pruned as marked

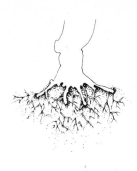

After pruning bushy new roots branch out

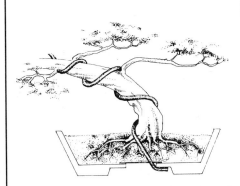

Binding with wire trains the bonsai trunk

Never wire tightly or loosely, but firmly

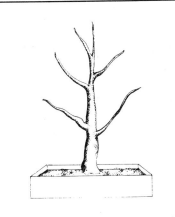

Upturned branches make a tree look young

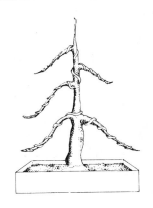

Correct this by wiring the branches down

must allow time for the plant to settle. Use copper wire—except for Cherry trees or young delicate shoots where pipe cleaners should be used. Do not wire unnecessarily and be careful not to damage the branch. Remove the wire as soon as the branch is set in its new position.

When wiring the trunk of the tree the end of the wire must be anchored so that it is taut enough to pull the trunk in the required direction. You can do this by inserting the wire through the drainage hole while you are repotting, and then leaving it on the surface of the soil until you are ready to wire the trunk.

Top pruning

Bonsai are pruned to give them shape and a bushy appearance. This should generally be done in spring. Never prune roots and the top growth at the same time, as this will give the plant too much of a shock.

Cut off the top tips to get a bushy look. And prune carefully to give the tree the desired shape. Think about the final shape you want the tree to have, and consider the angle from which it will be seen. (If you buy a ready-grown bonsai you will of course only have to trim it, its basic shape will have been established long before you bought it).

indoor hanging gardens and wall baskets

These look very pretty indoors if you can find a suitable spot to hang them. Light-loving plants will do well in a basket or bowl hung at a window from a curtain track if that is no longer used, provided the window does not get too much sun for their taste. In winter, it may be necessary to move it from such an exposed position. It all depends on what you are going to plant in it.

Baskets or other containers can be hung from the ceiling (if you can locate a joist into which to screw a hook), from wall brackets, or under an arch or in an alcove. In any position that is away from daylight, install a fluorescent tube at least 2 feet above, or choose shade-loving plants. The same applies to wall pots.

The most usual hanging container is a wire basket (which may have to be lined with plastic or foil for indoor use, to prevent drips), or a plastic one with drip-tray incorporated. Other possible containers are lined wicker baskets, gilded bird cages, or polythene bowls in which you can pierce holes for the hanging cords. Polythene is not a very attractive material but if the bowl is filled with hanging plants, it will soon be hidden. In a china bowl or ordinary flower pot an electric drill will make the holes needed for taking the cord or nylon thread by which to hang the 'garden' when it is ready.

For some situations, a long narrow container might be more effective, running right across a window, to screen an ugly view, for example. This will be heavy, so suspend it by chains from two brackets, one at each side of the window. Soilless compost is relatively lightweight but needs frequent watering unless planted with cacti or succulents that do not need much moisture.

If you line a wire basket with plastic or with foil folded double, choose trailing plants to conceal the lining and also puncture a few holes in it through which to push the roots of some small plants. Any container without a drainage hole must have a layer of charcoal chips at the bottom to absorb excess water. Then fill up with John Innes Compost No. 2.

After planting the basket and watering it, leave it in a cool place for a few days before hanging it up. Once a week it is likely to need water, with an addition of liquid fertilizer. Use very little water if there is no drainage hole. Judge how much to give as accurately as you can: hanging baskets are apt to lose a lot of moisture through evaporation. On the other hand, if there is no drainage hole, there is a greater risk of the compost getting soggy.

What plants to choose? Since you will be seeing the basket from below, trailing ones are an obvious choice; plus some to climb up the chains. Very small flowers will scarcely show. Here are some suggested combinations:

For a vivid and conspicuous display, a group of *Fuchsias* (including trailing varieties) on their own or with Asparagus Fern; or *Pelagorniums*, both upright and trailing; an *Impatiens* (Busy Lizzie); or, in softer tones of pink and green, a *Beloperone guttata* (Shrimp Plant).

For a cool white and green scheme, *Campanula isophylla alba* showering down, a *Philodendron* twining up the chains, and a *Chlorophytum comosum* (Spider Plant). This will do well even where light is limited.

A *Zygocactus* (Christmas Cactus) looks good in a smaller container, by itself as it needs much less water than most plants except in winter.

A permanent foliage group for a shady spot could be created with Mother-of-Thousands, Wandering Jew and Ivy (all these trail down but are of contrasting shapes, colours and textures) perhaps with a Pepper Elder, Asparagus Fern or Aluminium Plant in the middle. (In a group like this you could leave a permanent space for a small vase of flowers to give a point of colour, changed every week.)

A smaller, low-hanging container, perhaps in front of a blocked-in fireplace, could be filled with *Saintpaulias* (African violets); or (for the early part of the year only) indoor Primulas — they could be replaced with *Begonia semperflorens* in summer.

A group of Cacti or other succulents, needing little watering, could also be used.

In a big basket it is best to leave the plants in their pots, surrounding these with peat or moss. This makes it easy to rearrange them occasionally.

In addition, some attractive plants which will trail either stems and leaves or offsets over the edge of the basket or container include:

Bryophyllum crenata (yellow) and *B. uniflorum* (pinkish).

Crassula nealeana (yellow), *C. corallina* (yellow), *C. nemorosa* (pink) and *C. spatulata* (pink).

Indoor *Mesembryanthemums* such as *M. cooperi* (magenta), *uncinatum* (pink), *tortuosum* (pale yellow), *laeve* (yellow) and *turbinatum* (red).

Sedums such as Ruby Glow (pink), *album* (white), *reflexum* (yellow), *pulchelum* (purple), *hybridum* (yellow) and *sieboldii* (pink).

Two varieties of *Sempervivum: macedonicum* (red/purple) and *tectorum* (various colours).

Kleinia pendula (red/orange).

Additional suggestions for plants for hanging gardens and baskets include:

A collection of Heathers, which have leaves varying in colour from silver and gold to deep green, some with drooping stems, and which, by careful selection, can give a show of flowers at intervals throughout the year. There are many varieties to choose from, but a good mixture could include varieties of *Erica carnea*, *darleyensis* and *tetralix* — all giving flowers in a range of colours from white to pink to deep magenta. A compost without chalk is important for these plants, which like plenty of peat.

Bulbs for winter and early spring: Crocus, Snowdrops and double Tulips (using bulb fibre).

A mixed perennial basket consisting of trailing plants such as *Aubretia* (many of red, blue and purple colours), *Vinca minor* (Periwinkle) with its small green and whitish leaves, *Lysimachia nummularia* (Loosestrife) (gold leaves), and *Cerastium tomentosum* (Snow in Summer) (grey leaves and white flowers). All should be cut back with scissors or secateurs to keep them under control and to encourage free flowering and plenty of new, colourful leaf shoots.

Other plants useful for trailing or climbing include:

Ficus radicans, Ficus pumila, Chlorophytum capense, Fittonia verschaffeltii, Pellionia daveauana, Jasminum officinalis aurea variegata, Lonicera japonica variegata, Fuchsia procumbens (this has fascinating hip-like red fruits).

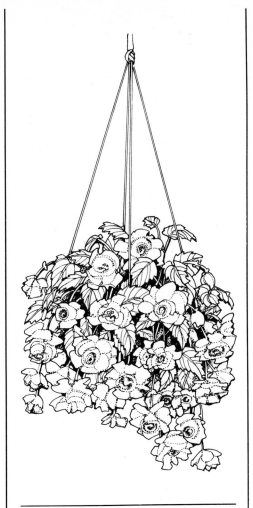

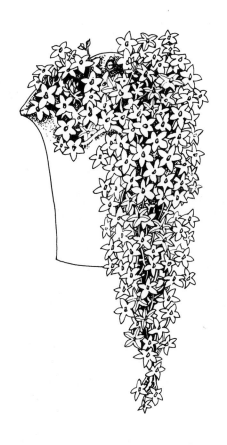

Begonias in a hanging basket
(above left)
Campanula isophylla hanging from a wall-
container (left)

A foliage group in a hanging
container. The long strands of ivy
trailing down help to create a
'floating' effect (above)

boxes, baskets and balconies

Window-boxes

Window-boxes serve two functions; the first is to decorate the outside of a house, thus giving pleasure not only to the owner but also to passers by, and the second is to add to the pleasure of those inside by giving them a tiny foreground landscape of flower and leaf through, or across, which to look at the world. The view through a window is much improved on a grey morning if it is seen past the nodding heads of Daffodils or Pot Marigolds.

How many boxes

The shape, size and number of window-boxes will, obviously, be dictated by the house itself. If you have just one window-box it should be colourful and well-tended—it must merit the attention it will undoubtedly receive. Alternatively, you could have a mixture of troughs, pots and window-boxes—each filled with different varieties of flower. Just think of those pavements, yards, and flights of steps in the Mediterranean countries where every kind of pot and pan, even painted petrol tins, contains a glittering cascade of bright flowers which enliven the dullest corner.

Types of window-box

Window-boxes can be found in many materials. They can either be bought ready-made or made to fit a particular window. The traditional wooden box is still a favourite and will last well provided it is painted with a preservative and one or two coats of paint. Good hard wood such as teak, elm, oak or red cedar can be treated with preservative and left to weather. The less heavy deal boxes need two or three coats of paint. White, off-white, or stone colours are usually good ones to choose. Or a dark blue, green or grey. It is probably best to avoid bright hues and to let the flowers provide all the colour.

How to make a window-box

If you want to make your own window-box choose wood ¾-1 inch thick. The usual length for a box is 3-4 feet, and the ideal width is 9-10 inches—certainly anything less than 7 inches is too narrow for the plants to be happy, and anything wider than 10 inches will hang dangerously far over most sills. The base of the box must have 1-inch drainage holes in it, each about 12 inches apart.

Fixing the box

Place strips of wood under the box to lift the base off the window-sill and allow air to circulate and water to drain away. The box must be very firmly attached to both the window-sill and wall. And, if there is a gap, drive wedges of wood between the end of the box and the wall.

Soil and planting

Before the box is filled with soil each drainage hole must be covered with a brocken crock, and a 1-2 inch layer of crocks and gravel spread over the bottom of the box. With window-boxes, as with any other pot or container, it is vitally important to use a really good soil. Fill the box up to about 1 inch from the top.

You can put the plants straight into the soil, or, if you prefer, you can put the plants in pots, put the pots in the window-box, and pack them around with soil and peat. This second method makes it easier to remove a plant if it dies, and also means that if you have sharp winters your favourite plants can be brought inside in their pots and put into the window-box again when all danger of frost is past.

When to plant

Plant window-boxes as you would plant a garden. Put in hardy plants in fine weather during winter and spring, sow hardy annuals in early summer or buy them later as plants. Bulbs should be put in in late summer or early autumn.

Which plants to choose

Plants in window-boxes tend to have a somewhat hard life, with periods of drought and wind, draughts and little protection. Certain hardy plants are, therefore, almost synonymous with window-box gardening. Choose *Chrysanthemum Frutescens* (Marguerites), *Petunias* double and single—flowery and floppy in glorious colours—*Lobelias* light and dark, *Fuchsias*, *Verbena*, *Begonia Semperflorens*, and, of course, the favourite flowering plants such as Geraniums and *Pelargoniums*. Miniature Roses, sharing with their fully grown relations a tough disposition, are also good in boxes, as are Hydrangeas. *Petunias*, Marigolds, *Lobelia*, and *Verbena* are happy in window-boxes which get a lot of sun. *Begonias* and Pansies will prefer a shadier spot.

Ideal for window-boxes, and as delightfully edible as they are decorative, are miniature Tomatoes with their marble-sized fruits. Team them with Green Beans, they have beautiful scarlet flowers and you could train them up the sides and around the top of your window, framing it completely. *Ipomoea* (Morning Glory) can be used for the same purpose as they, too, are good climbing plants.

Flowers all the year round

With some planning and re-planting a window-box can be kept flowering throughout most of the year.

You could start the box, with Bulbs and sweet-smelling Wallflowers and Forget-me-nots which will bloom when the Bulbs are over. When these are over why not put in *Nicotiana* (Tobacco)—

You can emphasise the angles of a roof with window-boxes, and bold pots of Geraniums lend drama to a balcony.

white to smell and lime green for the marvellous colour—with Pansies and, later, Nasturtiums with their brilliant flames and oranges.

A window-box of herbs
Sweet-smelling Rosemary and Lavender are good window-box plants, and if you have a convenient sill and are devoted to cooking have a box for more of your favourite herbs. Many useful ones—Chives, Chervil, Parsley, Savory, Thyme and Marjoram—will thrive in a box if they are kept well-watered.

Use of flower colours
A brighter, gayer and generally more daring use of colour is possible in a window-box because the flowers are contained in a rigid framework, be it lead, stone, wood or concrete (or the magic fibre-glass which can look like any of these) which effectively cuts them off from nature. What would be unthinkable in the way of colour combinations in a flower bed on a large scale becomes quite acceptable when in a box set off against stone or brick. Shocking, iridescent pink *Petunias* with orange Marigolds, for example, or vermilion Geraniums with velvety pink and purple *Pelargoniums*.

Although it is often highly successful to have a bright, multicoloured plant pattern in a box, it is also very effective to have shades of one colour, or one colour with white. Try planting yellow and orange Marigolds with silver grey foliage plants; pink and white *Petunias*; purple Heliotrope with mauve *Petunias* and blue *Ageratum;* or pink and white Geraniums with *Fuschias*.

Care of the plants
As with all flowering plants, but even more so as they are at eye level and more noticeable, take care to remove flower-heads as soon as they die, so that you get constant blooms to the end of the season. In the hottest and driest times of the year you must remember to water at least once, and probably twice a day (early in the morning and in the evening) as window-boxes tend to dry out quickly. During the summer you could add a plant food once every two weeks or so.

Window-boxes in winter
Try not to have a window box which contains only dry dusty soil and a few dead sticks. In winter either clear the box out or remove it entirely to renovate for next year. The soil in window-boxes needs to be replaced roughly once a year so this could be a good time to do it. Alternatively, you could fill the box with winter evergreens like small Junipers and Cypresses, and tough little Heathers and Ivies. Either move these into the garden in spring, or put your flowers among them.

Hanging baskets

A basket can look extremely attractive hanging in a porch, on a balcony, or under a verandah. Like window-boxes and pot plants, they are a way of compensating for the lack of a garden, so do try to put them where you will enjoy them from indoors—not where they are only visible from outside the house.

You can have hanging baskets indoors, but line them with green plastic or buy special watertight baskets which have their own interior draining devices—otherwise you will have drips all over the floor each time you water.

Size, soil and succour
The basket itself should be at least 9 inches in diameter, if it is smaller than this it will not really hold enough soil to keep many types of plant healthy. Ideally it should be 1-1½ feet in diameter and have a depth of 6-9 inches.

Hanging baskets are planted at the beginning of summer, to be hung up outside when all danger of frost is past. Make sure you hang them from a strong support, they can get very heavy. Line them with moss, this will help to retain as much water as possible, and then fill them with a mixture of peat and potting soil. They must not be allowed to dry out and in the driest weather must be watered twice a day. If possible, it is better occasionally to take the basket down and immerse it in water rather than water it overhead. If you have very leafy plants, *Zebrinas* for example, clean their leaves occasionally by spraying or wiping them.

Where to hang it
Site the baskets carefully so that they do not cut out any light from the house. They must also be easy to water, but not so low that they thump unwary heads and not where they may drip on the innocent caller.

Which plants to choose
Plants which trail naturally are best: Ivies, *Lobelias*, pendant *Begonias*, *Petunias*, *Zebrinas*, *Chlorophytum* (Spider Plant) and Geraniums (particularly the ivy-leaved varieties), with Nasturtiums sown among them to roar away at the end of the summer. Trailing *Fuschias* can look lovely, too, but they need plenty of space in which to grow and dislike draughts.

Balconies

For town-dwellers a balcony, if you are lucky enough to have one, offers an opportunity to create a miniature garden. Like window-boxes and hanging baskets a balcony can improve the dreariest outlook. It is so much nicer to look at green growing things and colourful groups of flowers than to be forced to stare at the windows of the house opposite.

Even on the smallest balcony (or flat roof) it is possible to use the space to grow decorative plants, and even useful plants like one or two pots of Tomatoes, or a big pot of Green Beans climbing up canes. If space is very limited, and the position is sheltered enough for them, make use of the wall by having climbing plants.

Some good annual climbers are *Cobaea Scandens* (the Cup and Saucer plant) which has greenish-white flowers changing to violet as the flowers mature, and can cover a wall in a summer as it grows up to 10 feet high up strings or a lattice; *Rudbekia Hirta* (Black-eyed Susan) which does best in semi-shade and is covered in vivid yellow flowers from mid-summer until autumn.

The most beautiful of all the annual climbers are, perhaps, the *Ipomoea* (Heavenly Blue or Morning Glory) which lives up to its name with its brilliant shining blue trumpets, climbs up canes or string and does best in a sheltered place with a great deal of sun, and *Passiflora Caerulea* (Passion Flower) which is equally delicate and has beautiful sculptural flowers. For a narrow

The fragrant herbs Rosemary and Lavender make ideal window-box plants.

little box or sink garden in a less
sheltered spot *Sempervivums* (House
Leeks) are lovely. They spread and
propagate themselves and are as tough
as you could wish. Other alpine-type
plants such as some of the *Saxifrages*
could be planted with them.

On a shady balcony you could grow
Begonias, *Fuchsias*, Ferns, and trailing
Vines, in pots and tubs. For a sunnier
spot *Petunias*, *Salvias* and Geraniums
will be happier.

Small conservatories

An attractive and unusual idea is to put
shelves across a bay window and have a
mixed group of flowering and foliage
plants. Outside you could have a window box so that the whole window is **a**
mass of growing things. (Not, of course,
if it is a darkish room or a room in
which people have to work.) A hall or
landing window is ideal for this.

On the shelves grow pots of Ferns,
Geraniums, *Tradescantia*, *Begonias*,
Hoyas, *Solanum*, and trailing Ivies.

Alternatively, if your house has a
verandah you could have this glassed in
and turned into a small conservatory,
giving yourself an extension to the
house—a garden room.

If this room receives a lot of sun you
could grow Cacti and other desert
plants. If it is warm but shady, receiving
little direct sun, create a jungle atmosphere. Grow *Begonias*, *Philodendrons*,
Monsteras, and some of the tropical
Ferns. Keep the humidity up by hosing
down a stone floor each day and leaving
it to steam-dry.

*Chives, Chervil, Parsley, Savory, Thyme
and Marjoram—all good window-box herbs.*

*Geraniums and Salvias fill a window-box while Tomatoes, Green Beans and Morning
Glories decorate a balcony. Above Petunias cascade from a hanging basket.*

Colourful plants grouped in a deep kitchen window can be used to shut out a dismal view (above). A hanging basket full of gay flowers adds to the rural charm of this house (below).

Hanging baskets, creeping plants and plants with sculptural shapes have been used in this small Victorian conservatory and combine to give it an authentic period atmosphere (right).

Almost anything—provided it is the right size—will make a good container. Large urns and pots, of glass or china, jardinières and cachepots are ideal for pot plants and large flower arrangements standing on the floor (left), while mugs, teapots, glasses and even kettles make unusual containers for cut flowers (right).

watering

When?

Plants don't need regular watering: they *do* need regular inspection, to see whether they need watering. In warm weather or the growing and flowering season, they should be examined daily, for water often vanishes fast at such times.

The first thing to observe is the plant itself. If its leaves are drooping and flabby to the touch, water is needed. (If they are yellow and falling off, the trouble is likely to be too much water rather than too little.)

A plant that seems to use up its water very fast may have grown too big for its pot: tip it out gently, and if the roots are compacted, give it a larger pot.

The look of the soil can be misleading, for you see only the surface. Either press your finger in, or insert a skewer and see whether it comes out clean or with damp soil on it. If no soil clings, the plant is dry and water is needed.

Lifting a pot gives a good clue: light weight means that water is lacking. Tapping the pot (if it is made of clay) provides another test: a ringing sound, rather than a dull one, indicates lack of water. Another method is to keep a pebble on the soil: turn it over, and if its underside is not damp, water the soil. You can also buy a special probe which shows on a dial just how moist the soil is.

How much?

A thorough watering occasionally is better than a little frequently. The latter moistens only the top of the soil and causes the roots to come towards the surface in search of it. Most plants can safely be plunged in a bucket of water for half an hour or until bubbles stop, then stood where the surplus water can drain out freely. This ensures that water does not merely run down the sides of the pot and out at the bottom, which is what may happen when using a watering can. Those plants which hate having their leaves splashed can be stood in a saucer of water for ½ hour, then drained. Wick-watering is another alternative: place pots round a large bowl of water and put a length of thick cotton or wool between each pot and the water, so that the plants can continuously absorb some water (a useful device when going on holiday). Use pebbles to anchor the cotton.

Most indoor plants need liquid fertilizer in the water during the growing period, because a pot holds little soil and the nutrients in it are usually exhausted quickly.

If you can collect rain water, this is better for plants than tap water. You can also use water-softening tablets or a handful of peat left in a can of water overnight if the water is very hard. The water you use should be at room temperature.

Drainage

Most plants dislike soggy soil — hence the advice elsewhere in this book to put pebbles or charcoal inside containers that lack drainage holes. For the same reason, do not leave a pot standing in a saucer full of water. It is better to keep pots on dishes or trays containing gravel, seashells, pebbles or anything else to raise them up a little.

Reducing water-loss

The soil of indoor plants is likely to dry up through evaporation, particularly where there is central heating or if they stand in sunshine. Plastic pots conserve moisture better than porous clay ones. Standing one pot within another is a help; and plants grouped together protect each other from evaporation. Pots standing inside other containers can be surrounded by moss or peat which is kept damp — another way to reduce moisture-loss and keep the leaves fresh with the aid of the water-vapour that will be given off.

Evaporation from the exposed surface of the soil can be reduced if this is covered with gravel, stone chippings (from an aquarium shop), peat or moss. Putting a transparent cover over the whole plant (even a plastic bag) is a useful temporary measure, particularly when going on holiday. Be sure the bag is fastened tightly to the pot, but not touching the leaves — use twigs to keep it away from them.

All but furry-leaved plants like to have their foliage sprayed (use a special trigger-spray which gives a fine mist, or else a clean squeezy bottle of the kind used for detergents). This not only helps to keep a slightly moist 'microclimate' around the plant, but drips on to the soil. It makes sense to take steps like these to reduce water-loss — not only for the sake of the plants, but to reduce your work in watering them.

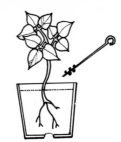

Insert skewer: if damp soil clings to it— no need to water yet

Or lift a pebble off: if underside is damp— no need to water yet

Roots too big for pot, so the plant will not get enough water

Light watering is bad. Roots turn upwards towards the surface

Water from can may run down edges of the pot and not through soil

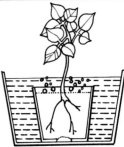

So leave the plant in a bucket of water until the bubbles stop

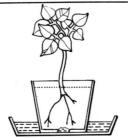

Or stand the plant in a saucer of water for about half an hour

Stand pots on pebbles to keep them clear of drips

When on holiday use cotton wick to convey water to plants

Moisture is conserved if pot is placed inside another container

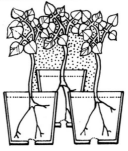

Plants grouped together help to conserve one another's moisture

Peat or moss around pots helps to reduce moisture loss

Cover soil surface with pebbles or stone chips to keep moisture in

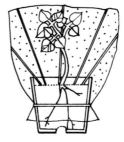

Plastic bag, kept off the leaves with twigs, conserves moisture

Spray foliage of all except the furry-leaved plants

propagating indoor plants

'Propagation' sounds very technical — yet getting two plants to grow where only one grew before is, in some cases, extremely easy if tackled in spring or autumn. One housewife who bought an Achimenes for a few pence turned out the dried-up remains months later, found 40 tiny tubers, put them in pots of compost in a warm place and had masses of blooms. She did the same again next year; and thus in two years got over 200 Achimenes! A massed effect of just one kind of plant can be very decorative.

Offsets

It is not only tubers like Achimenes that produce 'offspring'. Cacti and succulents have offsets, too; so do Mother-of-Thousands, Spider Plants, Bird's Nest Fern, Bromeliads, some Ivies, Mind-you-own-Business, Tradescantia, Zebrina, and many others. Gently separate the offspring from the parent, and put in another pot of damp compost. Protect from the cold (a plastic bag over the top will do) and await results.

Leaves

Some plants can be propagated by taking a single leaf and putting its stem into a pot of compost, sheltered by a plastic bag over the top. You can do this with *Saintpaulia*, (African Violet) Mother-in-Law's-Tongue, Pepper Elder and Dragon Plant (cut one leaf into several pieces) among others. *Begonia rex* leaves are treated differently. Lay one flat on compost, pinning it down with matchsticks or hairpins in several places. Small plants will start from these places.

Stems

In the case of many other plants, a piece of stem with several leaves on it is needed for propagation. Cut it slantwise just below a node, the little bump to be found below a leaf, a few inches from the top of the stem. Examples are Busy Lizzie, Pelargonium (Geranium), Wandering Jew, Aluminium Plant, Fittonia, Campanula, Fuchsia, Fat-Headed Lizzie, Fig, Coleus, Ivy Arum, Japanese Aralia, Jasmine, Kangaroo Vine, Solanum, and others. It is always worth trying this method with any plant. A stem of Ivy will also produce a new plant provided it has some root on it. Cover with a polythene bag, and leave in a warm shady place until the stem has rooted well.

Dividing

Some plants get quite bushy in a single season, and can be unpotted and gently pulled in two parts to plant separately. Also any others which look overcrowded or show signs of dying in the middle.

Give the plant plenty of water with fertilizer for a fortnight beforehand and keep it out of the sun to reduce transpiration. Cuttings, leaves or offsets can be taken the day before

A plant that is getting too dense and bushy will be improved by taking away its inward growing shoots and by removing dead leaves and flower heads

With a sharp blade cut top 3 inches off a strong shoot as shown in diagram, leaving a minimum of stump. Cut at angle so water will run off and just below a node (a little bump in the stem)

Remove all but the topmost leaves. Dipping the end of the stem in hormone rooting powder helps vigorous, healthy growth but is not essential. Plant without delay in damp compost

Peat pots make useful containers as they can go into other containers later. Cover cuttings with a plastic bag. They should not be exposed to sunshine and need little water until transplanted

When roots show through peat pots it is time to plant them into larger pots of compost (John Innes No1 or 2)

care

Before buying any plant decide exactly where you are going to stand it, and select one that will like the conditions it will get — sunny or shady, warm or cool. Few plants tolerate extremes or abrupt changes of temperature, so do not put them near fires or radiators, in draughts, or on window ledges where they may be sunburnt by day and chilled by night. All but a few need as much light as you can give them.

If you are going to mix several plants in one container, check also that they have the same needs where watering is concerned — or keep each in its pot within the larger container, and water each plant separately.

Potting

Most plants can be left, at least for their first season, in the pot in which they were bought, unless it is very small. But you may want to transfer a new plant to a trough or other container with other plants. (Even if left on its own, the plant may later outgrow its original pot. In any case, with time the nutrients in the original soil will be used up.)

A plant can be damaged in the course of transplanting it. It is usually best to do this in the early spring if possible, or autumn. First, the day before moving the plant to another container, water the compost thoroughly and leave it to drain for half an hour. The larger container should meanwhile be scrubbed clean if it needs it: a little permanganate of potash in the water will help to sterilize it. If a porous container is to be used, it should be soaked for a whole day first, otherwise it will take water away from the compost. Put ½ inch of compost in.

To remove the plant, place your hand over the top of the pot with the stem between your fingers. Turn the pot upside down, and the plant should come out into the palm of your hand, together with the ball of soil round its roots. A shake or a gentle tap on the edge of the table may be needed to free it.

Put the plant into the larger container: be sure the top of its soil ball is ½ inch below the rim of the pot, to allow space for watering. Fill up with compost to this level. Holding the plant steady, tap the pot on the table till the compost settles down (then add more, if necessary). Lightly press it down. Don't tamper with the soil ball, nor press the compost down hard, as this might injure the roots, and be sure that the compost is not covering much of the stem.

Some people put crocks in the bottom of the container before compost goes in. This is not essential but the drainage hole should be kept unclogged. Occasionally, push a pencil through it if necessary. If there is no drainage hole, then 1 inch of crocks, vermiculite or charcoal in the bottom of the container is necessary.

About compost

Different producers sell very different mixtures. To judge quality, look at the colour (it should be neither black nor too yellowy) and feel the texture (no large stones, worms, clods or weeds and not too sticky). If the bag is sealed, buy only a well-known brand. A good compost is, however, better than any soilless alternatives, for these tend to be very light and resistant to water once they have dried out.

John Innes Compost No. 2 is the one most often used for potting plants, containing enough nutrients for many weeks before fertilizer needs to be added. John Innes No. 3 is the richest in nutrients and no fertilizer need be added for the first season, but it should only be used for mature perennial plants: it is too strong for young plants.

Containers

You can use pots or boxes of any material that is rot-proof: metal (except zinc or untinned copper), china, glass, plastic, or even wood or wicker if lined with plastic or foil. The shape should relate to the shape of the plant: tall plants are apt to have long roots and need deep containers, spreading ones have spreading roots and need wide containers. Pot-bellied bowls present problems when repotting time comes, and therefore are best avoided. It is difficult to get the plant roots out through the mouth of such a bowl without damaging them.

It is more satisfactory to put several pots in one tray or trough rather than to dot them about separately. A grouping looks better, and makes for healthier plants. An inch of pebbles, vermiculite or peat and ½ inch of water in the bottom of the tray gives a humid but not soggy environment for the plants, and makes watering them much easier.

In a really deep trough, pots can be sunk in damp peat or vermiculite. Small ones can be raised to the rim of the trough by perching them on other empty pots stood upside down. Do not cover the bases of the stems, and be sure the larger pots are kept off the floor of the trough by a layer of pebbles or vermiculite. If the pots are clay and therefore porous, watering the peat or vermiculite will suffice; otherwise, water directly into each plastic pot. The latter method is better if you want to mix plants with different watering needs, whatever sort of pot.

After-care

The all-important subject of watering is dealt with in full later. Plants that get straggly will need to be trimmed, preferably after the flowering period, and tall ones may need to be lightly wired to a stick for support. Removing dead flowers and leaves is not only neat but it encourages fresh ones to grow. At the same time you can inspect for pests or disease and wipe dust off the leaves with a damp tissue.

Light

If you particularly want plants at some distance from a window, either pair them with others standing near the light and alternate their positions, or install artificial light about 2 feet above them. A warm-toned fluorescent tube is ideal because it does not overheat the plants as filament bulbs can do. It should be switched on for several hours a day, particularly in winter.

Conversely, if your plants must stand in a very sunny window, put up a blind or awning outside to protect them during summer.

Using a trolley as a plant stand is a good idea, for it can be moved when conditions get too hot or cold for the plants.

Feeding

Liquid fertilizers are the easiest type to use correctly. Overdosing can kill a plant. Add to the water, following the maker's instructions about quantity. Plants should be fed only during their growing and flowering period and not when they are obviously resting. When plants begin to die despite excellent care, it may be that residues of fertilizer (and of lime from hard water) are upsetting them, and it is time to re-pot in new compost.

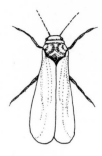

White Flies are tiny moth-like creatures who suck the sap of plants. The plant growth is weakened and the leaves look mottled and covered with a sticky film. Cure by spraying with insecticide.

Symptoms and diagnosis

If your plant looks unhealthy find the appropriate symptom below, and diagnose the cause of illness from the possibilities given. A sticky distorted look to the leaves, white webbing or mould probably means pest or disease has attacked.

Plants growing slowly

If a plant is growing very slowly or not at all during the summer—most plants of course would not be expected to grow in winter—it is probably either undernourished or overwatered. If you are watering and feeding it correctly then it could need re-potting.

Sudden dropping of buds, flowers or leaves

Usually this is caused by the plant having had too much water or a bad shock—a sudden drop or rise in temperature, a cold draught, extra light, or a change in its position.

Wilting

If leaves start wilting it could be that the plant is too hot or that there has been a sudden rise in the temperature. Alternatively it could be waterlogged because of over-watering, or simply dying of thirst. It should be easy enough to isolate which factor is responsible.

Yellowing leaves

It is normal for the occasional lower leaf to turn yellow and then fall off but if several do so a cold draught or over-watering is usually responsible. Alternatively if the leaves of lime-hating plants such as *Begonias* or Azaleas turn yellow but remain healthy this is usually a protest against the inclusion of lime in the potting compost or a sign that hard water (something else that they hate) has been used to water them.

Variegated leaves turning all one colour

If variegated leaves start to lose their stripes and markings it is only because the plant is not getting enough light. Move it to the window and the leaf colours will return.

Pests and diseases

Attack by pests or disease should be rare if your plants are well-tended and well-fed. But if they are attacked, prompt action can save them.

The common pests

Aphids (Greenfly) appear on the underside of leaves or on young shoots during spring and summer. The leaves look distorted and may fall off, and the whole plant has a sticky look. Cure by the sparing use of an insecticide safe for indoor use, or spray with weak soap flake solution once weekly, paying particular attention to the undersides of leaves.

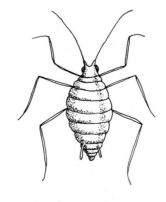

Scale Insects are tiny waxy shells. They cling to the stems and leaves of the shrubby plants and weaken them. Cure by rubbing off the insects with a matchstick tipped with cotton wool which has been dipped in methylated spirit.

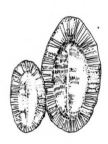

Red Spider Mites attack only under hot dry conditions. They damage the underside of leaves and sometimes leave a white webbing behind them. The tops of the leaves look grey and brittle. Cure by using a safe insecticide. Or try spraying the plant with water—red spiders hate water, and it will help the plant to breathe.

Mealy-Bugs are small, white and furry-looking. They appear in summer on the undersides of leaves and the joints of stems. Cure by treating as for scale insects.

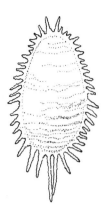

Thrips are tiny black flying insects which attack leaves and flowers leaving white dots and streaks in their wake. Cure by the sparing use of an insecticide which is safe for indoor use.

Humans are perhaps the most dangerous pest of all, insisting on touching and stroking leaves and flowers. Cure by discouraging them or, as a last resort, putting plants above their reach!

Diseases

In all cases cut out the diseased area immediately and move the diseased plant away from other healthy ones.

Rot usually attacks the roots and stems of plants and is often fatal. Cure by watering sparingly and keeping the plant in a reasonably warm room.

Mildew appears in summer in the form of white mould on the plant's stem and leaves. Cure by moving the plant to a well-ventilated spot. Check for possible overwatering as this can cause mildew.

Tiny round holes sometimes appear in a plant's leaves but apparently do not affect the health of the plant itself. Unfortunately there is no known remedy for this disease and, in fact, little is known about what causes it.

Causes of death

If a plant does die it is helpful to know, if possible, what caused its death so that you can avoid the same thing happening again. Causes of death are varied (and include attacks by the pests and diseases listed above) but the five most common ones are given below.

Drowning. Many plants, particularly in winter, die because they are drowned. Remember a wilted look could be due to overwatering as well as to thirst so before you water a wilted plant check whether the leaves are yellowish—too much water—or brown and shrivelled-looking—drought.

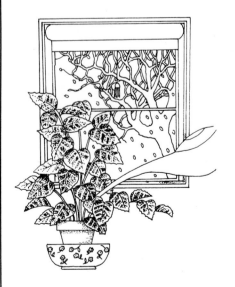

Drought. Obviously, no plant can survive without water, and remember that during the summer growing season a plant will need more water than it did during the winter.

Draughts. While many plants like fresh air most dislike draughts, particularly cold ones. Avoid putting a plant in a direct line between door and window, for when both are open an unpleasant crosscurrent will hit it. Make sure, too, that if you leave a plant on a window-sill throughout the winter there are no cracks in the window frame which will allow in icy draughts.

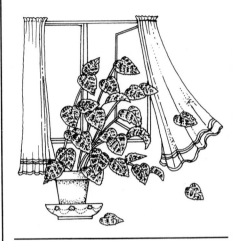

Lack of Humidity. Central heating, gas fires, and most other forms of artificial heat give a hot dry atmosphere. Plants then die through lack of humidity. (See pages 40-45 for how to overcome this problem.)

Lack of Light. Most plants, including the shade-lovers such as Ferns, will eventually die if they are kept in deep shade all the time. Plant symptoms of lack of light are no flowers or poor flowers on flowering plants, a weak stem, small pale leaves, and a leggy look to the plant as it strives to find the light.